The Doctrines and Discipline of the

Apostoic

Faith

Mission
of Los Angeles, California

The Doctrines and Discipline of the

Apostoic Faith Mission

of Los Angeles, California

THE COMPLETE AZUSA STREET LIBRARY

Volume 7

William J. Seymour

Series Compiled and Edited by

Larry E. Martin

RRMI CHRISTIAN LIFE BOOKS

THE PUBLISHING ARM OF RIVER OF REVIVAL MINISTRIES, INC.

John 7:38 PENSACOLA, FL 32516

ISBN 1-931393-33-8

CHRISTIAN LIFE BOOKS
P.O. BOX 36355
PENSACOLA, FLORIDA 32516
WWW.RRMI.ORG
WWW.AZUSASTREET.ORG
WWW.JESUS-IS-THE-ANSWER.COM

email: info@azusastreet.org

Dedication

This reprint is dedicated to Glenn A. Gohr,
a Christian, a Pentecostal historian, an archivist
and a friend.

THE DOCTRINES
AND
DISCIPLINE

OF THE

AZUSA STREET
APOSTOLIC FAITH
MISSION

Of Los Angeles, Cal.

1915

WITH SCRIPTURE READINGS

BY

W. J. SEYMOUR

ITS FOUNDER AND GENERAL OVERSEER

The Original Cover of *The Doctrine and Discipline*

The Larry Martin Collection

Contents

List of Illustrations

Foreword

Both *Life* magazine and *USA Today* list the Azusa Street Revival as on of the top 100 events–not just Christian, but nation impacting events–of the twentieth century. Led by a one-eyed, mostly self-educated son of former slaves named William J. Seymour, the Azusa Street Revival attracted men and women of every race, culture and walk of life, from across the United States and around the globe, to a converted livery stable on Azusa Street in Los Angeles, California. Frank Bartleman, on of the contemporaries of the revival, wrote about the Azusa Street Revival, "The color line was washed away by the blood." From those humble beginnings, nearly every major Pentecostal denomination was born, and can trace their roots, either directly or indirectly, to that three-year, nonstop revival.

This tremendous book, the information of which has been lost to the masses for many years, gives you unique insight into the heart and mind of the man through whom it all began, William Joseph Seymour, whom I believe to be one of the greatest men of the twentieth century, and in some ways, modern history. Due to racial pressures and social moors of the day, the revival ended with those same whites and blacks who came together in spiritual unity going their separate ways and beginning separate denominations, split along racial lines. In 1922, Bishop Seymour died quite literally of a broken heart. Until recent years, we didn't even know where he was buried. Much of our Pentecostal history, particularly surrounding Bishop Seymour, was obscured, buried and lost for many years, and is only now resurfacing. This is particularly significant among African-Americans, who, for so long, didn't realize what a major role they played in the revival that swept the world and is still impacting the planet in unprecedented measure with over 400 million Christians worldwide professing the baptism with the Holy Spirit with the evidence of speaking in other tongues.

Larry Martin, who has been my friend for over 20 years, is compiling a virtual library of twentieth century Pentecostal roots and history. This book is a powerful and informative addition to Pentecostal library. Recapture the origins of modern day Pentecost through the pages of this book, and learn not only what we believe, but why we believe it.

Bishop Carlton Pearson
Presiding Bishop, Azusa Fellowship International

Carlton wrote this foreword before his departure from traditional Pentecostal doctrines and practices. Our prayer is that our dear brother will return to the biblical view of redemption and Christianity that he once believed and preached so passionately.

Preface to the Series

The twentieth century Pentecostal/Charismatic movement was born on the first day of the last century, January 1, 1901, in Topeka, Kansas. For several months, the fledgling faith slept like a babe in a crib. Then for a couple of years she crawled around in Kansas, Missouri and Texas. In April 1906, Pentecostalism stood to her feet in a dilapidated old mission at 312 Azusa Street in Los Angeles, California. Once standing, the movement swiftly ran around the world. More than one hundred years later she is still running strong as revival fires fall fresh on a hungry church.

This series of books is about the Azusa Street Revival that started it all. These books are not conjecture or hearsay. These are primarily eye witness accounts and material from original sources. Although these witnesses may lie silent in the grave, their testimonies live to speak to a new generation hungry for a move of God.

There are two primary reasons why I have collected and published this material. First, before any of these testimonies are scattered and forgotten, I want to establish a record for the future. A record that is available not only in libraries and archives, but accessible to all Spirit-filled believers, clergy and layman, who want to relive their heritage. The Pentecostal/Charismatic church must never forget what happened at 312 Azusa Street.

Secondly, I pray that the reading of these dramatic stories will create a hunger in the hearts of the people of God. Although the United States has experienced some revival in recent years, we have seen nothing that equals the Azusa meeting and the impact it had on the world. If the church is going to survive around the world, we must pray for a fresh outpouring for a new millennium.

This project was started with the assumption that I would publish one book, erroneously believing that only a little material would be available. Now, I have collected the material for twelve books. Future editions will be published as the Lord wills and He provides the resources.

I have attempted to leave the record intact as much as was possible. In some cases, I have had to condense and to a very limited extent I have corrected misspelling (especially proper names) and punctuation. I have also changed the grammatical style (quotation marks, etc.) of some writers for the sake of consistency. In no instance did I add or subtract anything that changed the accuracy of the witness' account. If I have added editorial comments within the text, they are placed in brackets "[ ]" to distinguish them from the author's or editor's original comments that may be in parenthesis "( )."

I pray that my desire to present the original accounts as they were written will not cause any to be offended. Blacks are generally referred to as "colored" and some other language might not be considered appropriate by today's standards. Please remember that what is not acceptable today was the norm one hundred years ago. As you read, you will find that in most cases, the same language was used by both blacks and whites. In no case, is it my desire to offend. In fact, my prayer is that once again the children of God might worship together as one, regardless of race, ethnicity or affiliation. The "color line" is still washed away by Jesus' precious blood.

I am especially grateful to the guardians of our history for their diligence, without which this series would be impossible. I have studied at libraries, museums and archives from one end of this country to another. I could never thank every one who has contributed. Nevertheless, I must mention Assemblies of God archivist Glenn Gohr. His valuable assistance has greatly enhanced all of my projects. Also, this entire collection owes a great debt to Douglas J. Nelson the first Azusa Street scholar and Cecil M. Roebeck the most persistent.

A special thanks also goes to the many who provided me with materials and photographs with permission to reprint. Credit is given in the appropriate places. The entire series is better because of their generosity. I am also grateful to David Coleman for his excellent illustration for the cover.

This book is volume seven in the series. Volume one, *The Life and Ministry of William J. Seymour* is the foundation for the series. To fully understand the revival, it is a "must" read. The next three volumes contain testimonies of believers. Volumes five through seven are primary source materials that support the revival position. Volumes eight and nine capture the voices of the skeptics–religious and secular. The books of Frank Bartleman make volumes ten through twelve

As far as we know, this volume, a book of church polity and doctrine is the only literature produced directly by William J. Seymour, pastor of the Apostolic Faith Gospel Mission at 312 Azusa Street in Los Angeles, California. Yet, this valuable book has been seen by very few people, especially in the last seventy years. A few copies have survived, but they are in the hands of archives or collectors who have not made them available to the general public.

Christian Life Books is now pleased to present this reprint as an integral part of **The Complete Azusa Street Library**. It is important to note that this book is not being released because it is an especially great piece of literature, but because of its immense historical value. Although some sections contain Seymour's original thought and style, most of the discipline was borrowed from other works. Seymour copied many pages directly from **The Doctrine and Discipline of the African Methodist Episcopal Church**, making only a few omissions and additions where his on doctrinal preferences demanded it.

William Seymour was the son of slaves, reared in abject poverty in Reconstruction Louisiana. Although he attended school (probably the Freedman's Bureau) as a boy, he had little formal education. As a young man, Seymour was employed as a hotel waiter, a vocation that demanded no academic preparation.

In his early ministry, Seymour affiliated with the Church of God Reformation (Evening Light Saints). He would most certainly have encountered leaders who looked at theological education with a jaundiced eye.

Seymour attended a short-term Bible school in Houston, conducted by Charles F. Parham. He was only in the school for a few weeks and suffered the humiliation of sitting in the hall way outside the segregated class room, because of his color. Other than this, nothing is known of his religious training. One could fairly safely assume that for the most part he was self taught.

Seymour's grammar was poor and the order in which he collected materials seemed to have neither rhyme not reason. This presented a real challenge to me, as editor. I wanted to maintain the integrity of his work, while making the book palatable for modern readers. In some cases, I changed Seymour's writing. This was limited, however, to grammatical errors, verb tenses, etc. In no case did I omit anything or change the obvious meaning of any statement. Readers who are fanatical for the proper English will perhaps wish I had taken more liberties in my corrections, while the strictest of historians will wish that I had corrected nothing.

I altered the arrangement of the book, trying to assemble the material in an orderly fashion. Again, I omitted nothing. I also tried to classify the various subjects under topics, such as doctrine, family, etc. Some of the material is in narrative form, while other is outlined, probably depending on the source from which it was borrowed. I felt this was "clumsy" but I did not try to change it. In some cases, I did change the form of the outline only for the sake of consistency.

When I first published this book, I was set back by the amount of criticism I received from Pentecostal historians and acadamia. They did not think the original should be altered at all. Yet, among all these critics not one of the loquacious complainers had taken on the project and the necessary investment to publish the original. Ten years later they still haven't.

In spite of these difficulties, I feel the re-release of this book has made a valuable contribution to the study of Pentecostal history and especially the Azusa Street experience. From the original material, the reader will learn about Seymour and the mission. Even the borrowed material will give the reader insights into what the leader of the revival saw as important in his ministry and that of his followers.

The "glory" days at Azusa Street were from 1906-1909. There were times during this season that hundreds of visitors packed the mission almost every day and night. Pilgrims came from all over the world to share in the mighty outpouring of God's Spirit. By the time this discipline was published, however, Azusa was little more than a small congregation meeting in a dilapidated old building. The spotlight had moved to other more spectacular venues. Occasionally, visitors would drop by to see the place where "the fire fell" and reminisce about the revival. Seymour, while still pastoring the mission with his wife Jennie, was traveling into other areas of the country and even establishing several small churches in the East. In Seymour's mind, this may have created the need for the discipline's publication.

The reader will find some of Seymour's positions extreme and in some cases radical. His views on marriage and divorce were controversial in his day and will certainly continue to be so. Christian Life Books does not endorse all of the doctrinal positions espoused in this book and warns the reader to use caution if adopting any of the extreme points of view and to measure this and all works of man by the greatest standard, God's holy word.

I owe a special debt of gratitude to Jim Zeigler, former archivist at Oral Roberts University's Holy Spirit Research Center. He was the first to tell me about the discipline and shared a copy with me.

May God bless you as you read this book and dig deeper into the unique experience of what the pioneers called "Old Azusa."

Finally, let us all pray that the love, humility, tears, hunger and Pentecostal power that were the spirit of Azusa will visit us again. Our world, our nation, our churches need Holy Ghost revival.

Larry Martin
Pensacola, Florida

William J. Seymour

Original 1915 Preface

"Thy testimonies are very sure: holiness becometh thy house, Lord, forever" (Psalm 93:5). God's church is holy. Holiness is her ornament. "And her merchandise and her hire shall be holiness to the Lord it shall not be treasured nor laid up: for her merchandise shall be for them that dwell before the Lord to eat sufficiently and have durable clothing" (Isaiah 23:18).

Bless his name, salvation lies in the blood of Jesus. He says, "Abide in me and I in you. The same will bring forth much fruits. If you love me, keep my commandments" (John 15). That is, abide in His Word and if we abide in His Word we are under the blood and it cleanses us from all sin. Bless God forever. Amen!

Sanctification means holiness. Holiness means purity. To be pure means to be sanctified. There is no life sweeter than holiness unto the Lord, for He is holy and therefore commands us to be holy. We must keep holy unto the Lord. This work must stand for everything that is in the Word of God. The power of the Holy Ghost

(Acts 2:1-4; Acts 10:44-48; Acts 19:1-6). "Ye shall know the truth and the truth shall make you free" (John 8:31-32).

We take members in our church on probation, but not unconverted persons. They must know God and have a desire to go on to perfection (Hebrews 6:1-4).

Wherever the doctrine of the baptism in the Holy Spirit will only be known as the evidence of speaking in tongues, that work will be an open door for witches and spiritualists and free loveism. That work will suffer, because all kinds of spirits can come in. The Word of God is given to holy men and women not to devils. God's Word will stand forever (1 Peter 22-23).

When we leave the Word of God and begin to go by signs and voices we will wind up in spiritualism. God's Word is God's law. The Holy Spirit came to give us power to stand on the infallible Word and overcome these false spirits.

I know since God has given me strength to write these rules we will understand each other better, trusting so by the good Lord.

After much work, God has enabled me to put forth this book with the rule and doctrine of our church. Many things put in this little book have done me good by studying them. I hope in the name of the Lord it may do all the readers of our work good.

W. J. Seymour
Los Angeles, California
1915

W. J. Seymour in his senior years
Photo used by permission
Dixon Pentecostal Research Center

Apostolic Faith Gospel Mission
312 Azusa Street - Los Angeles, California

Photo used by permission
Apostolic Faith International Headquarters
Portland, Oregon

William Joseph Seymour
Signature on Transfer of Right of Way to
Iberia, St. Mary, and Eastern Railroad Company of Louisiana
Franklin, Louisiana
October 24, 1912

The Apostolic Address

To the Members of the Apostolic Faith Church:

Dearly beloved brethren, we esteem it our privilege and duty most earnestly to recommend to you this volume, which contains the doctrines and disciplines of our church, both of which, we believe, are agreeable to the Word of God, the only and all sufficient rule of faith and practice. Yet the church, using the liberty given to it by its Lord, and taught by the experience of a long series of years and by observations made on ancient and modern churches, has from time to time modified its discipline so as better to secure the end for which it was cofounded.

We believe that God's design in raising up the Apostolic Faith Church in America was to evangelize over these lands. As a proof hereof we have seen since 1906 that time of an extraordinary work of God extending throughout all the United States and territories and throughout the whole world.

In 1906, the colored people of the city of Los Angeles felt they were led by the Holy Spirit that they decided to have Elder W. J. Seymour, of Houston, Texas, to come to Los Angeles, California, and give them some Bible teaching. He came February 22, and started February 24, 1906. From his teaching one of the greatest revivals was held in the city of Los Angeles. People of all nations came and got their cup full. Some came from Africa, some came from India, China, Japan and England.

Very soon division arose through some of our brethren, and the Holy Spirit was grieved. We want all of our white brethren and white sisters to feel free in our churches and missions, in spite of all the trouble we have had with some of our white brethren in causing diversion and spreading wild fire and fanaticism. Some of our colored brethren caught the disease of their spirit of division also. We find according to God's Word to be one in the Holy Spirit, not in the flesh; but in the Holy Spirit, for we are one body (1 Corinthians 12:12-14). If some of our white brethren have prejudices and discrimination (Galatians 2:11-20), we can't do it, because God calls us to follow the Bible (Matthew 17:8; Matthew 23). We must love all men as Christ commands (Hebrews 12:14). Now because we don't take them for directors is not for discrimination, but for peace. To keep down race war in the churches and friction, so they can have greater liberty and freedom in the Holy Spirit. We are sorry for this, but it is best now and in later years for the work. We hope every one that reads these lines may realize it is for the best; not for the worse. Some of our white brethren and sisters have never left us in all the division; they have stuck to us. We love our white brethren and sisters and welcome them. Jesus Christ takes in all people in His salvation. Christ is all and for all. He is neither black nor white man, nor Chinese, nor Hindu, nor Japanese—but God. God is Spirit because without His Spirit we cannot be saved (John 3:3-5; Romans 8:9).

We don't believe in the doctrine of the artificial dancing that lots of people are calling the Holy Ghost dancing. David danced before the Lord. He danced with all his might. The ark was a type of the presence of Christ. David, laying aside his royal majesty, and girdled himself with a linen ephod; this represented that he had come in the immediate presence of God as a sinner to humble himself; it represented that he was naked before the Lord, in his heart. He felt he could not be (afraid) to be humbled, because God had been merciful to them in returning His presence of the ark which meant his glory. So David danced before the Lord, not before the people, for a show or a form, but before the Lord. The people saw him, and his wife, but it was in God's presence, so everything we do must be to the glory of God.

We believe in rejoicing in the Holy Spirit. We believe in shouting and leaping as the New Testament endorses.

Sound Doctrine

We must have sound doctrines in our work. We don't believe that the soul sleeps in the grave until the resurrection morning. Next, we don't believe in being baptized in the name of Jesus only. We believe in baptizing in the name of the Father, and the Son, and the Holy Ghost, as Jesus taught His disciples (Matthew 28:19-20).

We do not believe in keeping Saturday as the Christian Sabbath. We do not believe in dipping a person three times in order that he may be properly baptized. We believe in burying the candidate once in the name of the Father, and in the Son, and in the Holy Ghost.

Amen. We don't believe in fleshly doctrine of the male and female kissing and calling it the "holy kiss." It hurts the cause of Christ, and caused our good to be evil spoken of. We believe in the holy brethren greeting the brethren, and the holy sisters greeting the holy sisters with a kiss.

Amended Articles of Incorporation
of the
Apostolic Faith Mission

Whereas, at a meeting of the members of the Apostolic Faith Mission, a corporation, regularly and legally called and held at the office of said corporation at 312 Azusa Street, City of Los Angeles, County of Los Angeles. State of California, on the 19th day of May, 1914, at the hour of 7:30 P.M. all of the members of said Apostolic Faith Mission in good standing being present and voting, it was determined by resolution passed and adopted by unanimous vote, duly recorded, to amend the articles hereto, to-wit: on the 24th day of April, 1907, duly filed in the office of the County Clerk of Los Angeles County, State of California; that said amended articles and the constitution which is a part of these articles of incorporation, as hereinafter set forth were read, duly considered and adopted by the members of said Apostolic Faith Mission; that at said time and place the said board of trustees of said Apostolic Faith Mission, at its meeting duly and regularly called, unanimously, adopt said hereinafter amendments including said constitution which are a part of these amended articles of incorporation.

Now, therefor, these amended articles of incorporation and constitution, witnesseth:

I

That the name of this corporation shall be the Apostolic Faith Mission and shall be carried on in the interests of and for the benefit of the colored people of the State of California, but the people of all countries, climes, and nations shall be welcome.

II

That the purpose for which this corporation is formed are to do evangelistic work, conduct, maintain, control, carry on, supervise and found missions and also revivals, camp-meetings, street and prison work in the State of California and elsewhere, by its members, and those who become members by compliance with the constitution and by-laws and the tenets and beliefs of the Apostolic Faith Missions; to establish Sunday schools, supervise and carry on apostolic endeavors. It shall have the power to acquire such real and personal property as may be necessary for its use in carrying out its purposes and objects, and dispose of the same when no longer necessary for its use. It shall have the power to encumber all property, both real and personal, owned by it, when deemed advisable so to do; and generally to perform all acts requisite and necessary to more fully carry out its purposes aforesaid.

III

That the place where the principal business of the corporation is to be transacted is the City of Los Angeles, County of Los Angeles, State of California.

IV

That the term for which this incorporation is to exist is fifty (50) years from and after the date of the original incorporation.

V

The number of its trustees shall be three or five, and the names and addresses of the undersigned, who are hereby named as trustees of the corporation for the first year after the filing of these articles are:

Spencer James, 1632 West 35th Place, Los Angeles, California

James Ross, 312 Azusa Street, Los Angeles, California

And the name and residence of the one appointed for the first two years is:

Richard Asbery, 312 Azusa Street, Los Angeles, California

And the names and residences of the ones appointed for the first three years are:

Rev. W. J. Seymour, 312 Azusa Street, Los Angeles, California

Jennie E. M. Seymour, 312 Azusa Street, Los Angeles, California

That the said trustees are to be selected in the manner provided for in the constitution and by-laws of the Apostolic Faith Church.

VI

That on the 19th day of May, 1914, in the City of Los Angeles, County of Los Angeles, State of California, an election was held for trustees; that said election was held in accordance with a resolution at the last regular prior meeting of the said Apostolic Faith Mission, held on the 12th day of June in the office of said Corporation at the City of Los Angeles, County of Los Angeles, State of California; that notice of such meeting for the election of directors or trustees was given to the members of said Apostolic Faith Mission; that a majority of the members of said corporation who were present voted at such election, and that the result thereof was that the trustees hereinbefore named were duly elected for the respective terms.

VII

That this corporation has no capital stock and is not formed for profit.

Constitution of the
Apostolic Faith Mission

Article A

Section 1. The name of this corporation shall be the "Apostolic Faith Mission."

Section 2. The objects of this corporation are set in "II" of the amended articles as above set forth.

Section 3. There shall be no political discussions or any other discussions contrary to the law of God. The bishop shall decide what discussions shall take place in the mission.

Article B

This mission shall have jurisdiction over all subordinate missions that may hereafter be formed or come under the supervision of this mission. It shall have the right and power of granting charters to subordinate missions hereafter formed, or of suspending or annulling or revoking the same for proper cause.

Article C

This mission shall be composed of one bishop, one vice bishop, one secretary, one treasurer, five trustees, three deacons, two deaconsesses, two elders, one superintendent of Sunday schools, one superintendent of apostolic endeavor. The bishop, vice bishop and trustees must be people of color.*

Article D

The mission shall hold its annual meeting on the first Monday in April at 7:30 P.M. of each and every year. There shall be such other meetings as the bishop may elect.

Article E

The elective officers shall be the board of trustees who are elected as follows: Two for one year, one for two years and two for three years. All to be elected by ballot or the yea or no. That said trustees have been elected as hereinbefore set forth. After the first year there shall be three trustees only. The bishop and wife shall be trustees for life.

Article F

The founder and organizer of the mission shall be the bishop. He shall be a colored person, thoroughly converted and sanctified.

Article G

The other officers, trustees and bishop, shall be appointed by the bishop and hold office during such time

---

*The original constituion did not have this provision. The first board of trustees was racially mixed. This change reflects the problems Seymour encountered with white men repeatedly trying to take the mission from him. *Ed.*

as the bishop may direct and be subject to removal by the bishop.

The bishop shall approve all members taken into this mission, grant charters, revoke charters, establish rules and discipline for the guidance of the mission. Preside and lead at all meetings. Appoint all officers except the trustees. Remove all officers except trustees and perform any and such other and further duties that may devolve upon him from time to time. The bishop and wife shall be trustees for life time. The bishop and wife shall be head trustees of the church. The bishop shall remove trustees only for failing to obey the laws and doctrines of the church.

The vice bishop shall be appointed by the bishop and he shall be a colored man who has served the mission faithfully and well. His duties are as follows: Upon the death, removal, resignation or disqualification of the bishop, the vice bishop shall succeed the bishop. The vice bishop shall assist the bishop as he may direct. Help the bishop ordain preachers of the gospel as well as missionaries.

The duties of the other officers shall be as the bishop may provide.

Article H

There shall be such other committees as the bishop may provide and from time to time select, all to serve under the direction of the bishop and in the interests of the mission.

Article I

There may be such other subordinate missions as may from time to time be established. That upon the written request of not less than twenty-five persons who are converted, a mission may be founded and established. There must be passed a resolution by said twenty-five persons to the effect that they desire to found an Apostolic Faith Mission. The resolution expressing their desire must be forwarded to this mission. If the bishop is satisfied with the resolution he may then proceed to grant a charter to said mission, which is all times under the control and supervision of this mission. When the said charter is granted, the said mission becomes a part of this mission.

Article J

The bishop shall have power to hear all matters pertaining to the expulsion of any member of said mission and of any subordinate mission.

The bishop shall have power to expel or suspend any member for any misconduct or for any violations of the scriptures. Every member against whom any charge is filed shall have a hearing before the bishop and two other members or officers chosen by the bishop. If after hearing the evidence the said member may be expelled or suspended from the mission if the bishop and one member so order. But no one shall be expelled or suspended from the membership without the bishop's consent.

Article K

This Constitution may be amended in the manner provided by the consent of the bishop or by-law.

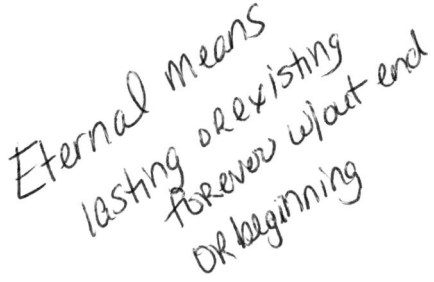

Eternal means
lasting or existing
forever w/out end
or beginning

Doctrines

The Apostolic Faith: A Doctrinal Overview

The Apostolic Faith stands for the restoration of the faith once delivered to the saints, the old-time religion of camp meetings, revivals, missions, street mission work and Christian unity everywhere. According to God's word (John 17:20,21).

Teaching on repentance (Mark 1:14,15).

Godly sorrow for sins (Examples: Matt. 9:13; 2 Cor. 7:9,11; Acts 3:19; Acts 17:30).

Confession of sin (Luke 15:21; Luke 18:13).

Restitution and faith in Jesus Christ (Ezek. 33:15; Luke 19:18).

Jesus died for our sins and arose for our justification (Romans 4:25).

The first work of grace. Justification is that act of God's free grace by which we receive remission of sins

(Rom. 3:25; Acts 10:42,43; Rom. 5:1,10; John 3:3,14; 2 Cor. 5:17).

The second work of grace. The Holy Ghost calls the second work the "second benefit." The margin reads "second grace." And the Syriac reads that you might receive the grace "doubly" (2 Cor. 1:15).

Sanctification is the second work of grace and is that act of God's grace by which He makes us holy in doctrine and life (John 17:15, 17; Heb. 13:12;2:11; Heb. 12:14). Jesus opened the Bible to his disciples before He went back to heaven (Luke 24:24-50). He taught His doctrine to them well before He went to Heaven so when we get sanctified Jesus will teach us the Bible also, bless the Lord.

Sanctification is cleansing to make holy. The disciples were sanctified before the day of Pentecost. By careful study of scripture, you will find it is so now. "Ye are clean through the word which I have spoken unto you" and Jesus had breathed on them the Holy Ghost (John 15:3; John 13-10; John 20:21,22). You know that they could not receive the Spirit if they were not all clean. Jesus cleansed and got all doubt out of His church before He went back to glory. The disciples had the grace of the Spirit before the day of Pentecost. The disciples had an infilling of the Spirit before the day of Pentecost. For Jesus had cleansed the sanctuary and they had the witness in their hearts that He was their risen Lord and Savior and they were continually in the temple praising and blessing God (Luke 24:51,53).

The baptism in the Holy Ghost and fire means to be flooded with the love of God and power for service, and a love for the truth as it is in God's word. So when we receive it we have the same signs to follow as the disciples received on the day of Pentecost. For the Holy Spirit gives us a sound mind, faith, love and power (2 Tim. 1:7). This is the standard Jesus gave to the church.

The greatest evidence of the Holy Spirit abiding in the believer is what Jesus Christ promised He would do. Jesus promised He would teach us all things, and bring all things to your remembrance whatsoever I have said so He means what He says. (John 14:17-26; John 16:7-15). So when He comes He does that in the believer, for He does it for me.

Seeking healing. We must believe, with great joy, that God is able to heal "I am the Lord that healeth thee" (Exodus 15:26; Jas. 5:14; Psalm 103:3; 2 Kings 20:5; Matt. 8:16,17; Mark 16:16-18). "Behold I am the Lord, the God of all flesh; is there anything too hard for Me?" (Jer. 32:27; Luke 24:52,53).

God, Spirit and Word go together. They are the two witnesses spoken of in Zech. 4:3-14 and Rev. 11:3. When these two witnesses are not recognized all kinds of confusion will be manifested in the church.

Too many have confused the grace of sanctification with the enduement of power or the baptism with the Holy Ghost. Others have taken "the anointing" which we receive after we are sanctified for the baptism and failed to reach the glory and power of a true Pentecost (John 20:21-24; Acts 2:3,4).

We read in the second chapter of Colossians, "Beware lest any man spoil you through philosophy and vain deceit, after the tradition of men, after the rudiments of the world, and not after Christ." This chapter tells us about Christ blotting out the handwriting of ordinances that were against us and contrary to us, and I am glad He did nail these ordinances to the cross with Him. He took them out of the way, nailing it to His cross. Bless the Lord. These were the old Jewish ordinances of divers washings, Sabbath days, new moons, circumcision and the Passover supper, and so on. But Jesus has ordinances in His church. Bless His dear Name.

Three ordinances Christ Himself instituted in His Church. First, He commands His ministers to baptize in water in the name of the Father and the Son and the Holy Ghost and it was practiced by the apostles (Matt. 28:19; Acts 32:38; Acts 22:16; Acts 8:12,17). The eunuch was baptized (Acts 8:35). The Apostle Paul was baptized. So many cases we can find in Acts where it was practised after John the Baptist had died.

We believe in water baptism. Our mode is immersion only, and single, in the name of the Father, and of the Son, and of the Holy Ghost. Matt. 28:19,20; 2 Cor. 13:13; and as much light as the Holy Ghost will reveal to us by His word.

Second, foot washing is an ordinance that Jesus Himself instituted in His church and we, His followers, should observe it. For He has commanded us to observe all things that He has commanded us to teach. So we find we will have to recognize these three ordinances.

We believe in the feet washing; we believe it to be an ordinance. Jesus said, in the John 13-17, "Ye call me Master and Lord, and ye say well, for so I am. If I then, your Lord and Master, have washed your feet, ye also ought to wash one another's feet for I have given you an example, that ye should do as I have done to you. Verily, verily I say unto you, the servant is not greater than his Lord: neither is he that is sent greater than he that sent him. If ye know these things, happy are ye if ye do them.

We believe in the ordinance of the Lord's supper, as it is set forth in 1 Cor. 11:2, 23-34 and Matt. 26: 26-29. We believe in taking unfermented wine and unleavened bread.

We the ministers, must be the husband of one wife (1 Tim. 3:2; Titus 1:6-9). We do not believe in unscriptural marriage (Rom. 7:2-4; 1 Cor. 7:39).

In Matt. 19:3-9, Matt. 5:32 and Mark 10:5-11, Jesus restored marriage back to the Edenic standard. Many are confused over the meaning of these passages. If either the husband or wife have defied themselves in the sins mentioned Jesus does not give either recognition as being legally married, while the first husband or wife is still living. They must repent to God and be reconciled to each other "for as Christ forgives so must we forgive" (1 Cor. 7:11). If a man or woman marry and either one has a living husband or wife their continuing to live together is a committing of fornication or adultery and the party who has a living husband or wife should be put away by the other, leaving the man or woman who has no living companion free to marry again to some one who is also free (1 Cor. 7:2; Matt. 19:9).

We do not believe in making a hobby of this doctrine of divorce, but we believe in the truth by comparing scripture with scripture, that no one in this work can marry the second husband or the second wife, while the first one is living (Rom. 7:2,3,4; 1 Cor. 7:10,11; 1 Cor. 7:39; 1 Tim. 3:9; Matt. 5:32; Luke 16:18; Mark 2-12).

Bishop Hurst says, in his Church History, that the gift of tongues has appeared in communities under powerful religious stimulus, as among the Cornisards, early Quakers, Lasare in Sweden in 1841-43, in the Irish Revival in 1859, and in the Catholic Apostolic (Irvingite) Church (Vol. 1, page 90).

I can say, through the power of the Spirit, that wherever God can get a people that will come together in one accord and one mind in the Word of God, the baptism of the Holy Ghost will fall upon them, like as at Cornelius' house (Acts 10:45,46). It means, to be in one accord, as the word says in Acts 2:42,47.

The blood of Jesus will never blot out any sin between man and man they can make right; but if we can't make wrongs right, the blood graciously covers (Matt. 5:24; Matt. 6:15; Matt. 18:35; 1 John 1:7-9).

Dear loved ones, God's promises are true. We read in Exodus 12:3, God commanded Moses to take a lamb for a house and a house for a lamb when He was about to bring the children out of Egypt. Bless His holy Name, amen! They were to kill the lamb and take its blood and sprinkle it over the door overhead and the sides to save them from the destroyer. But in the very house they were instructed to eat the body. The blood saved them from the destroyer, but the body of the lamb saved them from disease and sickness. Glory to His Name! May we obey God's word and voice and we shall be saved through Jesus from sins and feast on His perfect body. Jesus is founder of His church, the Christian church, by His own precious blood. Hallelujah! So, Jesus is the Christian Passover. When the Jews eat the Passover they remember God bringing them out of Egypt and point to His coming. So we eat the Christian Passover and remember Calvary, how Jesus died and saved us, and we look forward to His coming again.

Moses' lamb was a type of Christ, the true Lamb, so Christ is our Lamb, bringing health to our imperfect body. Moses was founder of the Jewish church, by God, through the paschal lamb by the blood and body of the lamb. But Jesus is the Lamb of God, the founder of the Christian church.

Amended Articles of the Doctrines*

The Apostolic Faith Mission, 312 Azusa Street, stands for the following scriptural doctrines, ordinances, and truths, to-wit:

First, as amended: "Justification by faith, which we interpret as being the 'forgiveness of sins,' which is the 'new birth' spoken of in John 3:1-13" (Also Acts 10:42-43: Rom. 3:25). The doctrine of justification shall not be changed.

Second, as amended: "Sanctification by faith as a second definite work of grace upon the heart, which represents entire cleansing, made holy in heart" (John 17:15-17; 1 Thess. 4:3-5; Thess. 4:3; Heb. 2:11-13; Heb. 10:10; Heb. 13:12). The doctrine of sanctification cannot be changed.

Third, as amended: "The baptism with the Holy Ghost as a gift of power upon the sanctified life, and anointing for service and work" (Acts 2:1-4; Acts 10:45-46; Acts 19:6; 1 Cor. 4:21).

Fourth, as amended: "The speaking in tongues being one of the 'signs following' the baptized believers and other evidences of the Bible, casting out devils,

---

* This section was included in the original book with this heading, "Article V. as an additional piece to the Constitution, covering doctrinal points and articles of faith." In the index, it was listed as "Amended Articles of the Doctrines." *Ed.*

healing the sick and with the fruits of the Spirit accompanying the signs" (1 Cor. 13; Mark 16:16-19; Acts 2:2-3; Acts 10:44-45-46; Act 19:6).

Fifth, as amended: "We believe and teach that God intended and Jesus taught that there could be no holy union between man and woman after divorcement for any cause, so long as both parties to the first covenant live" (Mal. 2:14-17; Matt. 5:32; Matt. 19:3-9; Mark 10:11-12; Luke 16:18; Rom. 7:1-4; 1 Cor. 7:39).

Sixth, as amended: "We believe in the ordinance of 'water baptism,' and teach that immersion is the only mode, in the name of the Father and of the Son, and of the Holy Ghost, only one dip, in the name of the Trinity."

Seventh, as amended: "We believe in the ordinance of the Lord's supper as instituted by Jesus and followed by the apostles, and teach that it should be frequently observed in holy reverence."

We do not believe in baptizing babies or children before they come to the age of accountability. A little child cannot believe.

Eighth, as amended: "We believe in feet washing as an ordinance, as it was established by our Master before the Lord's supper, according to John 13:4-18, and believe it was practiced by the Apostles and disciples through the First Century" (1 Tim. 5:10).

To belong to this faith they must obey its teachings.

Propositions and Statements

Proposition 1. The Bible is a Divine Revelation given of God to men and is a complete and infallible guide and standard of authority in all matters of religion and morals; whatever it teaches is to be believed, and whatever it commands is to be obeyed; whatever it commends is to be accepted as both right and useful; whatever it condemns is to be avoided as both wrong and hurtful; but what it neither commands nor teaches is not to be imposed on the conscience as of religious obligation.

Proposition 2. The New Testament is the constitution of Christianity, the charter of the Christian church, the only authoritative code of ecclesiastical law, and the warrant and justification of all Christian institutions. In it alone is life and immortality brought to light, the way of escape from wrath revealed, and all things necessary to salvation made plain; while its messages are a gospel of peace on earth and of hope to a lost world.

We must take the Bible as the infallible word of God (Luke 24:25-31; Luke 24:44-45; John 5:39).

Proposition 3. None but regenerated persons ought to be, or properly can be, members of a Christian church, which is a spiritual body separate from the world and distinct from the state and to be composed of spiritual members only.

Proposition 4. Christ is the only Head over and Lawgiver to His church. Consequently the church cannot make laws, but only execute those which He has given. Nor can any man, or body of men, legislate for the church. The New Testament alone is their statute book, by which, without change, the body of Christ is to govern itself.

Articles of Religion

1. Of Faith in the Holy Trinity. There is but one living and true God, everlasting, without body or parts, of infinite power, wisdom and goodness; the maker and preserver of all things, visible and invisible. And in unity of this Godhead there are three persons, of one substance, power, and eternity–the Father, the Son, and the Holy Ghost (Matt. 28:19-20; 1 John 5:6-9).

2. Of the Word, or Son of God, who was made very Man. The Son, who is the Word of the Father, the very and eternal God, of one substance with the Father, took man's nature in the womb of the blessed virgin: so that two whole and perfect natures, that is to say, the Godhead and manhood, were joined together in one person, never to be divided; whereof is one Christ, very God and very man, who truly suffered, was crucified, dead and buried, to reconcile His Father to us, and to be a sacrifice, not only for original guilt, but also for the actual sins of men.

3. Of the Resurrection of Christ. Christ did truly rise again from the dead, and took again His body, with all things appearing to the perfection of man's nature, wherewith He ascended into heaven, and there sitteth until He returns to judge all men at the last day.

4. Of the Holy Ghost. The Holy Ghost, proceeding from the Father and the Son, is of one substance, majesty, and glory with the Father and the Son, very and eternal God.

5. The Sufficiency of the Holy Scripture for Salvation. The holy scriptures contain all things necessary to salvation; so that whatsoever is not read therein, nor may be proved thereby, is not to be required of any man that it should be believed as an article of faith, or be thought requisite or necessary to salvation. In the name of the holy scriptures we do understand those canonical books of the Old and New Testament of whose authority was never any doubt in the church. The names of the canonical books are:

Genesis, Exodus, Leviticus, Numbers, Deuteronomy, Joshua, Judges, Ruth, The First Book of Samuel, The Second Book of Samuel, The First Book of Kings, The Second Book of Kings, The First Book of Chronicles, The Second Book of Chronicles, The Book of Ezra, The Book of Nehemiah, The Book of Esther, The Book of Job, the Psalms, The Proverbs, Ecclesiastes or the Preacher, Cantica or Song of Solomon, Four Prophets the greater, Twelve Prophets the less.

All the books of the New Testament, as they are commonly received, we do receive and account canonical.

6. Of the Old Testament. The Old Testament is not contrary to the New; for both in the Old and New Testament everlasting life is offered to mankind by Christ, who is the only Mediator between God and man, being both God and man. Wherefore they are not to be heard who feign that the old fathers did look only for transitory promises. Although the law given from God by Moses as touching ceremonies and rites doth not bind Christians, nor ought the civil precepts thereof of necessity be received in any commonwealth; yet, notwithstanding, no Christian whatsoever is free from the obedience of the commandments which are called moral.

7. Of Original or Birth Sin. Original sin standeth not in the following of Adam (as the Pelagians do vainly talk) but it is the corruption of the nature of every man, that naturally is engendered of the offspring of Adam, whereby man is very far gone from original righteousness, and of his own nature inclined to evil, and that continually.

8. Of Free Will. The condition of man after the fall of Adam is such that he cannot turn and prepare himself, by his own natural strength and works to faith, and calling upon God; wherefore we have no power to do good works, pleasant and acceptable to God, without the grace of God by Christ preventing us, that we may have a good will, and working with us, when we have that good will.

9. Of Justification of Man. We are accounted righteous before God only for the merit of our Lord and Saviour Jesus Christ, by faith, and not for our own works or deservings. Wherefore, that we are justified by faith only is a most wholesome doctrine, and very full of comfort.

10. Of Good Works. Although good works which are the fruits of faith, and follow after justification, cannot put away our sins, and endure the severity of God's judgments: yet are they pleasing and acceptable to God in Christ, and spring out of a true and lively faith, inasmuch that by them a living faith may be as evidently known as a tree is discerned by its fruit.

11. Of Works of Supererogation. Voluntary works—besides, over, and above God's commandments—which are called works of supererogation, cannot be taught without arrogance and impiety. For by them men do declare that they do not only render unto God as much as they are bound to do, but that they do more for His sake than of bounden duty is required; whereas Christ saith plainly. When ye have done all that is commanded of you, say, We are unprofitable servants.

12. Of Sin after Justification. Not every sin willingly committed after justification is the sin against the Holy Ghost, and unpardonable. Wherefore, the grant of repentance is not to be denied in such as fall into sin after justification.

After we have received the Holy Ghost, we may depart from grace given, and fall into sin, and by the grace of God, rise again and amend our lives. And therefore they are to be condemned who say they can no more sin as long as they live here; or deny the place of forgiveness to such as truly repent.

13. Of the Church. The visible church of Christ is a congregation of faithful men in which the pure word of God is preached, and the sacraments duly administered according to Christ's ordinance, in all those things that of necessity are requisite to the same.

14. Of Purgatory. The Romish doctrine concerning purgatory, pardon, worshiping and adoration, as well as images as of relics, and also invocation of saints, is a fond thing, vainly invented, and grounded upon no warrant of scripture, but repugnant to the word of God.

15. Of Speaking in the Congregation in such a Tongue as the People Understand. It is a thing plainly repugnant to the word of God, and the custom of the primitive church, to have public prayer in the church, or to administer the sacraments, in a tongue not understood by the people (1 Cor. 14:1-33).*

16. Of the Sacraments. Sacraments ordained of Christ are not only badges or tokens of Christian men's profession, but rather they are certain signs of grace, and God's good will toward us, by the which He doth work invisibly in us, and doth not only quicken, but also strengthen and confirm, our faith in Him.

There are three sacraments ordained of Christ our Lord in the gospel; that is to say, baptism and the Lord's supper and feet washing.**

---

* This should be understood as a reference to the Roman Catholic traditon of Latin mass, not speaking in tongues. *Ed.*
** Seymour modifed this section to include foot washing.

The sacraments were not ordained of Christ to be gazed upon, or to be carried about; but that we should duly use them. And in such only as worthily receive the same they have a wholesome effect or operation; but they that receive them unworthily, purchase to themselves condemnation, as St. Paul saith (1 Cor. 11: 29).

17. Of Baptism. Baptism is not only a sign of profession and mark of difference whereby Christians are distinguished from others that are not baptized; but it is also a sign of regeneration or the new birth. *

18. Of the Lord's Supper. The supper of the Lord is not only a sign of the love that Christians ought to have among themselves one to another, but rather is a sacrament of our redemption by Christ's death; insomuch that, to such as rightly, worthily and with faith receive the same, the bread which we break is a partaking of the body of Christ; and likewise the cup of blessing is a partaking of the blood of Christ.

Transubstantiation, or the change of the substance of bread and wine in the supper of our Lord, cannot be proved by Holy Writ, but is repugnant to the plain words of scripture, overthroweth the nature of a sacrament, and hath given occasion to many superstitions.

The body of Christ is given, taken, and eaten in the supper, only after a heavenly and spiritual manner. And the means whereby the body of Christ is received and eaten in the supper is faith.

The sacrament of the Lord's supper was not by Christ's ordinance reserved, carried about, lifted up or worshiped.

---

*Seymour ommits a sentence the Methodists added on the baptism of children.

19. Of both Kinds. The cup of the Lord is not to be denied to the lay people; for both the parts of the Lord's supper, by Christ's ordinance and commandment, ought to be administered to all Christians alike.

20. Of the one Oblation of Christ, finished upon the Cross. The offering of Christ, once made, is that perfect redemption, propitiation and satisfaction for all the sins of the whole world, both original and actual; and there is none other satisfaction for sin but that alone. Wherefore the sacrifice of masses, in the which it is commonly said that the priest doth offer Christ for the quick and the dead, to have remission of pain or guilt, is a blasphemous fable and dangerous deceit.

21. Of the Marriage of Ministers. The ministers of Christ are not commanded by God's law either to vow the estate of single life, or to abstain from marriage; therefore it is lawful for them, as for all other Christians, to marry at their own discretion, as they shall judge the same to serve best to godliness (1 Tim. 4:1-7).*

22. Of the Rites and Ceremonies of Churches. Whosoever, through his private judgment, willingly and purposely doth openly break the rites and ceremonies of the church to which he belongs, which are not repugnant to the word of God, ought to be rebuked openly (that others may fear to do the like), as one that offendeth against the common order of the church, and woundeth the consciences of weak brethren.

23. Of Christian Men's Goods. The riches and goods of Christians are not common, as touching the right, title and possession of the same, as some do falsely boast. Notwithstanding, every man ought, of such things as he posseseth, liberally to give alms to the poor, according to his ability.

---

*Seymour elimnated a statement "Of the rulers of the United States."

24. *Of a Christian Man's Oath.* As we confess that vain and rash swearing is forbidden Christian men by your Lord Jesus Christ and James His apostle; so we judge that the Christian religion doth not prohibit, but that a man may swear when the magistrate requireth, in a cause of faith and charity, so it be done according to the prophet's teaching, in justice, judgment and truth.

God

God is a Spirit (John 4:24; 2 Cor. 3:17). He is declared to be:
1. Invisible (Job 23:8,9; John 1:18; John 5:37; Col. 1:15; 1 Tim. 1:17; 1 Tim. 6:16).
2. Eternal (Deut. 33:27; Psalm 90:2; Rev. 4:8-10).
3. Immortal (1 Tim. 1:17).
4. Incorruptible (Rom. 1:23).
5. Omnipotent (Gen. 17:1; Rev. 19:6).
6. Omnipresent (Psalm 139:7-10; Jer. 23:23).
7. Omniscient (Psalm 139:1-6; Prov. 5:21).
8. Immutable (Psalm 102:2,6,27; Jas. 1:17).
9. Only-wise (Rom. 16:27; 1 Tim. 1:17).
10. Incomprehensible (Job 36:26; Job 37:5; Isa. 40:18; Micah 4:12).
11. Unsearchable (Job 11:7; Job 26:14; Job 37:23; Isa. 40:28; Rom. 11:33).
12. Most High (Acts 7:48; Psalm 83:18).
13. Love (1 John 4:8,16).
14. Perfect (Mat. 5:48).
15. Holy (Psalm 99:9; Isa. 5:16).
16. Just (Deut. 32:4; Isa. 45:21).
17. True (Jer. 10:10; John 17:3).
18. Upright (Psalm 25:8; Psalm 92:15).
19. Righteous (Ezra 9:15; Psalm 145:17).
20. Good (Psalm 25:8; Psalm 119:68).
21. Great (2 Chr. 2:5; Psalm 86:10).

22. Gracious (Ex. 34:6; Psalm 116:5).
23. Faithful (1 Cor. 10:13; 1 Pet. 4:19).
24. Merciful (Ex. 34:6,7; Psalm 86:5).

The Soul of Man

The soul is the real man (Matt. 16:26). For what is a man profited if he gain the whole world and lose his own soul or what shall a man give in exchange for his soul? And fear not them that kill the body but are not able to kill the soul; but rather fear him which is able to destroy both soul and body in hell (Matt. 10:28). The soul stands for the whole man. It is immortal and immaterial. But yet man himself is a trinity. He is a trinity like his maker. Consisting of spirit, soul and body (1 Thess. 5:23). And the very God of peace sanctify you wholly; and I pray God your whole spirit and soul and body be preserved blameless unto the coming of our Lord Jesus Christ. Faithful is He that calleth you, who also will so it. So we see that we are spirit and soul and body.

The soul stands for the whole man because it will be required at the judgment. Thou fool, this night thy soul shall be required of thee (Luke 12:20).

Since man fell he has a perfect salvation granted him through Jesus Christ for spirit, soul and body (1 Thess. 5:23). So, when speaking about the eternal existence of man, we say his soul.

The spirit, the higher nature of man is that which knows God (John 3:5-6). Jesus answered, "Verily, verily I say unto thee, except a man be born of water and of the Spirit he cannot enter the kingdom of God. That which is born of the flesh is flesh; that which is born of the Spirit is Spirit. Therefore it is through the Spirit that we know God (John 4:24). God is a Spirit and they that worship Him must worship Him in Spirit and in truth. The Spirit is man's higher nature which knoweth God and communes with God by the Spirit. Before we can know God we must repent of our sins and accept Jesus and be born of the Spirit. Then we can know God for we have His Spirit to witness with our Spirit that we are the sons of God. The Spirit Itself beareth witness with our Spirit, that we are children of God (Rom. 8:16). The spirit is the higher nature of man which knows God, distinguishes between right and wrong and is capable of religious affections, emotions and exercises. This is spiritual life.

Man a Trinity

The highest life a man can live is to commune with God, being born again and being filled with God's Spirit.

Man, according to the Bible philosophy, is a trinity like his creator, consisting of spirit, soul and body (1 Thes. 5:23). And the very God of peace sanctify you wholly; and I pray God your whole spirit and soul and body be preserved blameless unto the coming of our Lord Jesus Christ.

Faithful is he that calleth you, who also will do it (Heb. 4:12).

The word of God is quick and powerful, and sharper than any two-edged sword, piercing even to the dividing asunder of soul and spirit and the joints and marrow, and is discerner of the thoughts and intents of the heart. Neither is there any creature that is not manifest in His sight (Heb. 4:12,13). Man is a trinity. The spirit is his higher nature, that which knows God and distinguishes between right and wrong. Adam knew right from wrong because as soon as he did wrong he hid himself from the presence of God (Gen. 2:17; Gen. 3:7).

The spirit is the higher nature of man, capable of religious affections, emotions and exercise. The physical is the other extreme. It is the earthy part of man, material organism indwelt by the soul. They are tied together with spirit and the instrument of its desires, purposes and operations. Intermediate between these is the soul, the rational mind–the seat of the affections; the understanding; that which loves and hates; that which can discriminate; that which thinks; that which can be cultivated and which has at once its lower passion and its fined tastes.

The physical man is the man that is controlled by the physical nature. There are three conditions in which we may live. First, we may be controlled by our lower nature, our animal life or existence–our body and its gross appetites. This is pure sensuality, the real flesh life, the fruit of the flesh (Gal. 5:19-21).

Secondly, we can be controlled by our intellectual department, our tastes–by our intelligence and our affections and passions; the proud and haughty physical nature. If a man is controlled by his intelligence, it makes him proud many times. If he is controlled by his mind alone, he will be heady and high minded. He will be nice but in his heart he will be proud. Nothing can atone for him but the blood of Jesus Christ, the Son of God.

Thirdly, he may be controlled by his spiritual nature. This will be quite different. The man that is controlled by his intellect will be worldly minded. His mind must be fed. How? By the material things–shows, picnics, card parties, dances and big dinners. The natural man is controlled by his natural mind. He cannot help it because he was born after the fallen Adam. He must be born again (John 3:3). Behold I was shapen in iniquity and in sin did my mother conceive me (Psalms 51:5; Psalms 58:3).

Since all three departments of man's nature are fallen and under the curse, he needs the blood of Jesus Christ. When a man is born again he is a new creature (2 Cor. 5:17). Old things are passed away, all things have become new.

Since the three departments are fallen we need to turn the whole man over to God (1 Thes. 5:23). All of these departments are tied together by the almighty God. His body is mortal; His spirit is immortal.

It seems that the soul stands for the entire man or the whole man–believing to the saving of the soul (Heb. 10:39). "What will it profit a man if he gain the whole world and lose his own soul."

Temptations are great but the blood is sufficient for every trial. If we yield to the bodily appetites, we become sensual; if we yield to those of the mind, we become worldly minded, and if we yield to an evil spirit we become devilish. May God help us to become strong and arm ourselves against the flesh (Eph. 6:10,11).

We must remember that every man that is born in the world is lame in his intellect, will and affections. He must be born again and get sanctified and get filled with the Holy Ghost and go on to perfection (Heb. 6:1-4). That is the only safeguard for Christians.

Many churches today get a physical preacher to preach about Christ and many of them know nothing about Christ because they have not been born again.

The Bible teaches that a man must be born again (John 3:3).

We learn from the Bible that a man must be holy to see God (Matt. 5:8). In Christ's first sermon on the mount, He preached holiness (Matt. 5:8; Matt. 5:20; Matt 5:48). Holiness, without which no man shall see the Lord (Heb. 12:14). Many people today go to church and just hear a physical sermon and come back no better in their soul that they were before going. God help us. Amen.

The New Birth

Salvation comes through the blood of Jesus Christ. When we get it, we will know it, and if we lose it we will know it. There is only one way to get it–by repenting and believing the gospel. (John 3:5,6; Rom. 8:7,8; Titus 3:5; Mark 1:15).

Salvation is not feeling; it is a real knowledge by the Holy Spirit, bearing witness with our spirit (Rom. 8:14-16). Jesus said to Pontius Pilate, when Pilate asked him if He then was a king [Apparently something is missing in this sentence, perhaps a printing error–*Ed.*]. Since Jesus had told him that He had a kingdom, but His kingdom was not of this world, so Pilate believed if He was a king then He had a kingdom.

Jesus told him His kingdom was not of this world. He said, "If My kingdom was of this world then would My servants fight, that I should not be delivered to the Jews; but now is My kingdom not from hence." Pilate asked Him about His kingdom and kingship, so He confessed He was a king over His people in the Holy Spirit, for He said: "To this end was I born, and that I should bear witness unto the truth." So when we get the salvation of God into our hearts we will bear witness to the truth–not lies. But like the disciples on their way to Emmaus when Jesus met them and spoke about the truth, their hearts bore witness to the truth (Luke 24:13-32).

Some people today cannot believe they have the Holy Ghost without some outward signs; that is heathenism. The witness of the Holy Spirit inward is the greatest knowledge of knowing God, for He is invisible (St. John 14:17). It is all right to have the signs following, but not to pin our faith to outward manifestations. We are to go by the word of God. Our thought must be in harmony with the Bible or else we will have a strange religion. We must not teach any more than the apostles (1 Cor. 12:1-34; 1 Cor. 13:1-13; 1 Cor. 14:1-40).

Justification and Sanctification

Our doctrine on justification and sanctification, as definite works of grace cannot be changed.

The Plan of Salvation

The plan of salvation is already laid, so we can do nothing to improve it. It is fixed for all eternity. We are to accept it as it is. When we set up our own standard of holiness for God to work by, we dishonor God and set up an idol in our hearts. When we do this, also we tell God in the way we act that we won't hear His word without Him coming to our terms. God wants us to have faith to take Him at His word. So many people have made shipwreck of their faith by setting up a standard for God to respect or come to.

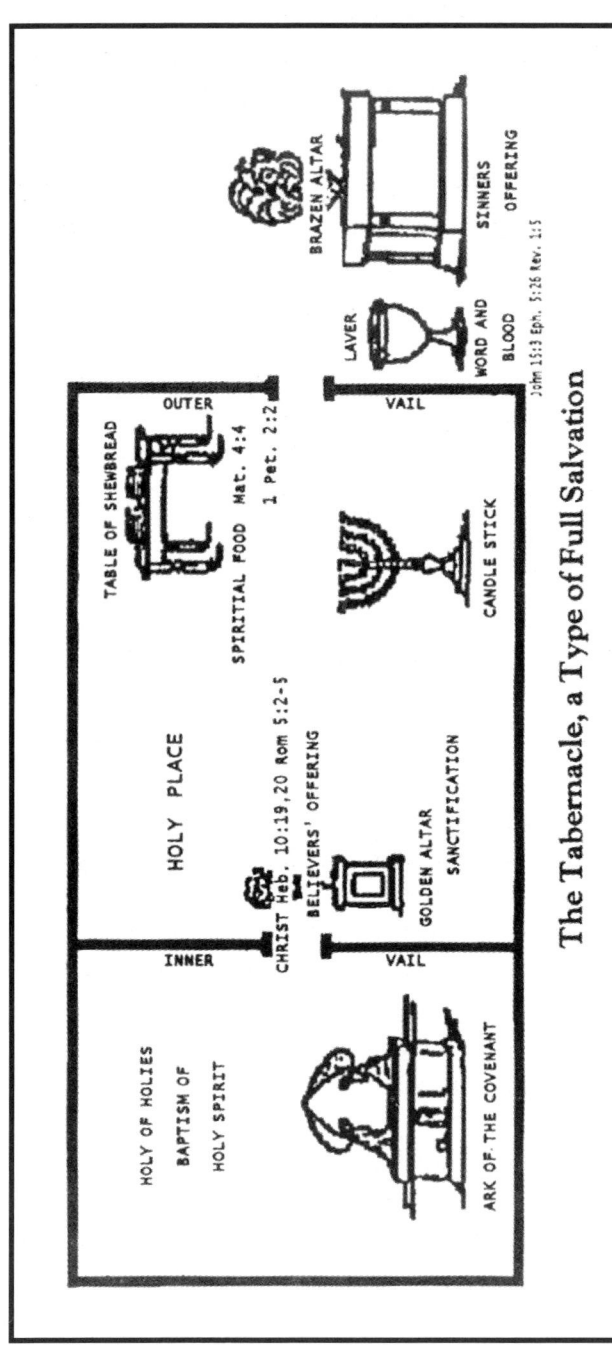

The Tabernacle, a Type of Full Salvation

(This illustration was on page 11 of the original book)

The Inner Witness

How would a man know that he was born of the Spirit, if he did not have the inward witness? He would have to look for some outward sign. But God's word says he that believeth on the son of God, hath the witness in himself (1 John 5:10).*

Melchizedek

I. He was a man–a priest (Gen. 14:18)

II. He was a type of Christ (Heb. 5:6)

III. Neither Melchizedek nor Christ were united to the Jewish priesthood (Psalms 110:4; Heb. 7:21; Zech. 6:13)
1. He was ordained direct from heaven (Gen.14:18)
2. Christ our high priest came into office the same way (John 8:54; Heb. 5:5; Acts 3:13)
3. Melchizedek's descent was not counted from Levi and Aaron (Heb. 7:6)
4. Neither was Jesus Christ's (Heb. 7:11, 19; Gal. 2:21; Heb. 8:7)
5. Christ was not of the tribe of Levi, nor of the family of Aaron, but of Judah (Heb. 7:10-14)
6. There was no record kept of Melchizedek's or Christ's birth, parentage, and death, according to the Jewish custom (Heb. 7:3)

IV. The Lord had a people on earth before he called Abraham from or out of the Chaldeans (Gen. 12:1; Gen. 15:7; Gen. 5:22)

---

*In the original, this section on the inner witness appeared under the heading "Support for the Ministry." *Ed.*

V. The calling of Abraham was for a special purpose (Gen. 17:6; Gen. 12:1,2; Gen. 22:18; Gen. 26:4; Gal. 3:8)

VI. There was no Mosaical law when God called Abraham (Heb.11:9; Gal. 3:17; Rom. 5:13,14; Deut. 5:2, 3)

VII. The plan of salvation did not come through the Sinaiaitic code (Gen. 17:4; Rom. 4:13; Gal. 3:27)

VIII. The law of grace is separate from the law of Moses (Rom. 4:14-18; John 15:22; John 1:17)

Catechism on Faith
Part One

Question 1. What is it to be justified?
Answer. To be pardoned and received into God's favor, into such a state, that if we continue therein, we shall be finally saved.

Question 2. Is faith the condition of justification?
Answer. Yes, for every one that believeth not, is condemned; and every one who believes, is justified (Rom. 5:1-3).

Question 3. But must not repentance and works meet for repentance, go before this faith?
Answer. Without doubt; if by repentance you mean conviction of sin, and by works meet for repentance, obeying God, forgiving our brother, leaving off from evil, doing good, and using his ordinances according to the power we have received.

Question 4. What is faith?

Answer. Faith in general is a divine, supernatural evidence, or conviction of things not seen, not discoverable by our bodily senses, as being either past, future or spiritual. Justifying faith implies not only a divine evidence or conviction that God was in Christ, reconciling the world to Himself, but a sure trust and confidence that Christ died for my sins, that He loved me and gave Himself for me. And the moment a penitent sinner believes this, God pardons and absolves him.

Question 5. Have all Christians this faith? May not a man be justified and not know it?

Answer. That all true Christians have such faith as implies assurance of God's love, appears from Rom. 8, 15:2; 2 Cor. 8:3; Eph. 4:32; Heb. 8:10; 1 John 4:10, 19. And that no man can be justified and not know it (St. John 3:11; 1 John 5:10). Faith after repentance, is ease after pain, rest after toil, light after darkness. It appears also from the immediate, as well as the distant fruits thereof.

Question 6. But may not a man go to heaven without it?

Answer. It does not appear from Holy Writ that a man who has heard the gospel can, whatever a heathen may do (Mark 16:16 Rom. 2:14-16).

Question 7. What are the immediate fruits of justifying faith?

Answer. Peace, joy, love, power over all outward sin, and power to keep down inward sin.

Question 8. Does anyone believe who has not the witness in himself, or any longer than he sees, loves and obeys God?

Answer. We apprehend not seeing God being the very essence of faith; love and obedience being the inseparable properties of it.

Question 9. What sins are consistent with justifying faith?

Answer. No wilful sin. If a believer wilfully sins, he casts away his faith. Neither is it possible he should have justifying faith again without previously repenting (Heb. 6:1,4).

Question 10. Must every believer come into a state of doubt or fear or darkness? Will he do so unless by ignorance or unfaithfulness. Does God other wise withdraw Himself.

Answer. It is certain a believer need never come again into condemnation. It seems he need not come into a state of doubt or fear or darkness, and that (ordinarily at least) he will not unless by ignorance or unfaithfulness. Yet it is true, that the first joy seldom lasts long: that it is followed by doubts and fears; and that God frequently permits great heaviness before any large manifestation of Himself.

Question 11. Are works necessary to the continuance of faith?

Answer. Without doubt; for many forfeit the free gift of God, either by sins of omission or commission.

Question 12. Can faith be lost for want of works?

Answer. The more we exert our faith, the more it is increased. To him that hath shall be given (Matt. 25:29). *

---

* Question 13 is missing in the original. *Ed.*

Question 14. Paul says, Abraham was not justified by works; James, he was justified by works. Do they not contradict each other?

Answer. No. First, because they do not speak of the same justification. Paul speaks of that justification which was when Abraham was seventy-five years old, about twenty-five years before Isaac was born. James of that justification, which was when he offered up Isaac on the altar. Second, because they do not speak of the same works. Paul speaking of works that precede faith; James, of works that spring from it.

Question 15. In what sense is Adam's sin imputed to all mankind?

Answer. In Adam all die (i.e., Rom. 5:12). First, our bodies then become mortal. Second, our souls died (i.e., were disunited from God). And hence, third, we are all born with a sinful, devilish nature. By reason whereof, fourth, we are children of wrath, liable to death eternal (Rom. 5:18; Eph. 2:3).

Question 16. In what sense is the righteousness of Christ imputed to all mankind, or to believers?

Answer. We do not find it expressly affirmed in scripture, that God imputes the righteous of Christ to any; although we do find that faith is imputed to us for righteousness. The text, "As by one man's disobedience, many were made sinners, so by obedience of one, many were made righteous," we conceive, means, by the merits of Christ all men are cleared from the guilt of Adam's actual transgression. We conceive further. Through the obedience and death of Christ, first, the bodies of all men become immortal after the resurrection. Second, their souls receive a capacity of spiritual life and third, an actual spark or seed thereof. Fourth, all believers become children of grace reconciled to God, and fifth are made partakers of the divine nature.

Question 17. Have we, then, unawares, leaned too much towards Calvinism?
Answer. We are afraid we have.

Question 18. Have we, not also leaned too much towards Antimonianism?
Answer. We are afraid we have.

Question 19. What is Antimonianism?
Answer. The doctrines which make void the law through faith the Doctrine of Antimonianism is so close to the perfect law of grace until we have to look closely to know the difference it says all Jesus . . . therefore Christians are not obliged to observed it; Third, that*

Question 20. What are the main pillars thereof?
Answer. First, that Christ abolished the moral law. Second, that one branch of Christian liberty is liberty from obeying the commandments of God. Fourth, that it is bondage to do a thing because it is commanded, or forbear because it is forbidden. Fifth, that a believer is not obliged to use the ordinances of God to do good works. Sixth, that a preacher ought not to exhort to good works–not unbelievers, because it is hurtful, not believers, because it is needless.

---

*The answers to questions nineteen and twenty are edited in a way that leaves the reader confused. Seymour added some presonal comment to answer 19 and then adds part of a sentence that was originally in Wesley's answer twenty. This leaves both answers awkward and incomplete. *Ed.*

Question 21. What was the occasion of Paul's writing his epistle to the Galatians?

Answer. The coming of certain men amongst the Galatians, who taught, "Except ye be circumcised and keep the law of Moses, ye cannot be saved."

Question 22. What is the main design herein?

Answer. To prove, first, that no man can be saved, or justified by the works of the law, either moral or ritual. Second, that every believer in Christ is justified by faith without the works of the law.

Question 23. What does he mean by the works of the law (Gal. 2:16,etc.)?

Answer. All works which do not spring from faith in Christ.

Question 24. What by being under the law (Gal. 3:23)?

Answer. Under the Mosaic dispensation.

Question 25. What law has Christ abolished?

Answer. The ritual law of Moses; not the moral law, for every believer keeps this moral law in his heart.

Question 26. What is meant by liberty (Gal. 5:1)?

Answer. Liberty, first from the law, second, from sin.

Part Two

Question 1. How come what is written on justification is so intricate and obscure? Is this obscurity from the nature of the thing itself, or from the fault or weakness of those who generally treated about it?

Answer. We apprehended this obscurity does not arise from the nature of the subject; but partly from the extreme warmth of most writers who have treated it.

Question 2. We affirm that faith in Christ is the sole condition of justification. But does not repentance go before that faith? Yea, and, supposing that there be opportunity for them, fruits or works meet for repentance? *Answer.* Without any doubt they do.

Question 3. How then can we deny them to be conditions of justification? Is not this a mere strife of words? *Answer.* It seems not, though it has been grievously abused. But so the abuse cease, let the use remain.

Question 4. Shall we read over together Mr. Baxter's aphorism's concerning justification? *Answer.* By all means.

Question 5. Is an assurance of God's pardoning love absolutely necessary to our being in His favor? Or may there possibly be some exempt cases? *Answer.* Yes.

Question 6. Is such an assurance absolutely necessary to inward and outward holiness? *Answer.* Yes.

Question 7. Is it indispensably necessary to final salvation? *Answer.* Love hopeth all things. We know not how far any man may fall under the case of invincible ignorance.*

---

*Question 8 is omitted in the original. *Ed.*

Question 9. Does a man believe any longer than he feels reconciled to God?

Answer. We conceive not. But we allow there may be infinite degrees of seeing God; even as many as there are between him that sees the sun, when it shines on his eyelids closed, and him who stands with his eyes wide open in the full blaze of his beams.

Question 10. Does a man believe any longer that he loves God?

Answer. In no wise. For neither circumcision nor uncircumcision avails, without faith working by love.

Question 11. Have we duly considered the case of Cornelius? Was he not in the favor of God when his prayer and alms came up for a memorial before God (i.e. before he believed in Christ).

Answer. It does seem that he was in some degree. But we speak not of those who have heard the gospel.

Question 12. But were those works of his splendid sins?

Answer. No; nor were they done without the grace of Christ.*

Question 16. Can faith be lost through disobedience?

Answer. It can. A believer first inwardly disobeys, inclines to sin with his heart; then his intercourse with God is cut off (i.e., his faith is lost). And after this he may fall into outward sin, being now weak and like another man.

Question 17. How can such a one recover faith?

Answer. By repenting and doing the first works (Rev. 2:5; Hebrews 6:1-3).

---

*Questions 13-15 are omitted in the original. *Ed.*

Question 18. Whence is it that so great a majority of those who believe, fall more or less in doubt or fear?

Answer. Chiefly from their own ignorance or unfaithfulness: often from their own not watching unto prayer; perhaps from some defect or want of the power of God in the preaching they hear.

Question 19. Is there not a defect in us? Do we preach as we did at first? Have we not changed our doctrines? I am afraid we have preached too much on tongues being the evidence of the gift of the Holy Spirit instead as one of the signs following the believer (Mark 16:16-18).*

Answer. First, at first we preached almost wholly to unbelievers. To those, therefore, we spake almost continually of remission of sin through the death of Christ and the nature of faith in his blood. And so we do still among those who need to be taught the first elements of the gospel of Christ.

Second, those in whom the foundation is already laid, we exhort to go on to perfection (Heb. 6:1-6; Heb. 10:26-27).

Third, we now preach, and that continually, faith in Christ as our prophet, priest, and king; as least as clearly, as strongly and as fully, as we did several years ago.

Question 20. Do not some of our preachers preach too much of the wrath, and too little of the love of God?

Answer. We fear that they have leaned to that extreme, and hence some of their hearers have lost the joy of faith.

---

*The portion on speaking in tonugnes is not part of the original materials borrowed from John Wesley. It is out of place in the sequence of questons, but Seymour seems detirmined to deemphasize speaking in tongues as the only evidence of a Spirit-baptized believer. *Ed.*

Question 21. Need we ever preach the terrors of the Lord to those who know they are accepted of him?

Answer. No; it is folly so to do, for love is to them the strongest of all motives.

Question 22. Do we ordinarily represent a justified state so great and happy as it is?

Answer. Perhaps not; a believer walking in the light is inexpressibly great and happy.

Question 23. Should we not have a care of depreciating justification, in order to exalt the state of holy sanctification?

Answer. Undoubtedly, we should be aware of this, for one may insensibly slide into it.

Question 24. How should we avoid it?

Answer. When we are going to speak of entire sanctification, let us first describe the bliss of a justified state, as strongly as possible.

Question 25. Does not the truth of the gospel lie very near both Calvinism and Antinomianism?

Answer. Indeed it does, as it were within a hair's breadth; so that it is altogether foolish and sinful, because we do not altogether agree with one or the other, to run from them as far as we can.

Question 26. Wherein may we come to the very verge of Calvinism?

Answer. First, in ascribing all good to the free grace of God. Second, in denying all natural free-will, and all power antecedent to grace. And, third, in excluding all merit from man even for what he has or does by the grace of God.

Question 27. Wherein may we come to the edge of Antimonianism? (Antimonianism was a sect originated by John Abricola of Germany about the year 1535).

Answer. First, in exalting the merits and love of Christ; second, in rejoicing evermore.

Question 28. Does faith supersede (set aside the necessity of) holiness or good works?

Answer. In no wise. So far from it that it implies both, as a cause does its effects.

Part Three

Question 1. Can an unbeliever (whatever he be in other respects) challenge anything of God's justice?

Answer. He cannot, nothing but hell; and this is a point on which we cannot insist too much.

Question 2. Do we exempt men of their own righteousness, as we did at first? Do we sufficiently labor, when they begin to be convinced of sin, to take away all they lean upon? Should we not then endeavor, with all our might, to overturn their false foundation?

Answer. Yes. This was at first one of our principal points; and it ought to be so still; for till all other foundations are overturned, they cannot build on Christ (1 Cor. 3:1-16).

Question 3. Did we not then purposely throw them into convictions; into strong sorrow and fear? Nay, did we not strive to make them inconsolable, refusing to be comforted?

Answer. We did. And so should we do still; for the stronger the conviction the speedier is the deliverance.

And none so soon receive the peace of God, as those who steadily refuse all other comfort.

Question 4. What is sincerity?
Answer. Willingness to know and do the whole will of God. The lowest species thereof seems to be faithless in that which is little.

Question 5. Has God any regard for man's sincerity?
Answer. So far, that no man in any state can possibly please God without it; neither in any moment wherein he is not sincere.

Question 6. But can it be conceived that God has any regard to the sincerity of an unbeliever?
Answer. Yes, so much that if he perseveres therein God will infallibly give him faith.

Question 7. What regard may we conceive Him to have to the sincerity of a believer?
Answer. So much that in every sincere believer He fulfill all the great and precious promises.

Question 8. Whom do you term a sincere believer?
Answer. One that walks in the light, as God is in the light.

Question 9. Is sincerity the same with a single eye?
Answer. Not altogether: the latter refers to our intentions, the former to our will or desires.

Question 10. Is it not all in all?
Answer. All will follow persevering sincerity. God gives everything with it; nothing without it.

Question 11. Are not then sincerity and faith equivalent terms?

Answer. By no means. It is at least as nearly related to works as it is to faith. For example; who is sincere before he believes? He that then does all he can; he that according to the power he has received, brings forth fruits meet for repentance. Who is sincere after he believes? He that from a sense of God's love, is zealous of all good works.

Question 12. Is not sincerity what St. Paul terms a willing mind (1 Cor. 8:12)?

Answer. Yes, if the word were taken in a general sense; for it is a constant disposition to use all the grace given.

Question 13. But do we not then set sincerity on a level with faith?

Answer. No, for we allow a man may be sincere and not be justified, as he may be penitent and not be justified (not as yet) but he cannot have faith and not be justified. The very moment he believes he is justified (Rom. 5:1,12).

Question 14. But do we not give up faith and put sincerity in its place as the condition of our acceptance with God.

Answer. We believe it is one condition of our acceptance, as repentance likewise is. And we believe it is a condition of our continuing in a state of acceptance with God. Yet we do not put it in the place of faith. It is by faith the merits of Christ are applied to my soul. But if I am not sincere they are not applied.

Question 15. Is not this that going about to establish your own righteousness, whereof St. Paul speaks?

Answer. St. Paul there manifestly speaks of unbelievers who sought to be accepted for the sake of their own righteousness. We do not seek to be accepted for the sake of our sincerity; but through the merits of Christ alone. In deed, so long as any man believes he cannot go about (in St. Paul's sense) to establish his own righteousness.

Question 16. But do you consider that we are under the covenant of grace; and that the covenant of works is now abolished?

Answer. All mankind are under the covenant of grace, from the very hour that the original was made. If by the covenant of works you mean that of unsinning obedience made with Adam before the fall; no man but Adam was ever under that covenant, for it was abolished before Cain was born. Yet it is not so abolished, but that it will stand, in a measure, even to the end of the world: that is if we do this, we shall live; if not, we shall die eternally. If we do well we shall live with God in glory; if evil, we shall die the second death. For every man shall be judged in that, and rewarded according to his works.

Question 17. What means then; to him that believeth, his faith is counted for righteousness?

Answer. That God forgives him that is unrighteousness as soon as he believes, accepting his faith instead of perfect righteousness. But then observe universal righteousness follows though it did not precede faith?

Question 18. But is faith thus counted to us for righteousness, at whatever time we believe?

Answer. Yes. In whatsoever moment we believe all our past sins vanish away. They are as though they never had been, and we stand clear in the sight of God.

Question 19. Are not the assurance of faith, the inspiration of the Holy Ghost, and the revelation of Christ in us, terms of nearly the same import?

Answer. He that denies one of them, must deny all; they are so closely connected.

Question 20. Are they ordinarily, where the pure gospel is preached, essential to our acceptance?

Answer. Undoubtedly they are, and as such to be insisted on in the strongest terms.

Question 21. Is not the whole dispute of salvation by faith, or by works, a mere strife of words?

Answer. In asserting salvation by faith we mean two things. First, that pardon (salvation begun) is received by faith, producing works. Second, that holiness (salvation continued) is faith working by love. Third, that heaven, (salvation finished) is the reward of this faith.

If you assert salvation by works, or by faith and works, mean the same thing, (understanding by faith, the revelation of Christ in us, by salvation, pardon, holiness, glory) we will not strive with you at all. If you do not, this is not a strife of words, but the very vitals, the essence of Christianity is the thing in question.

Question 22. Wherein does our doctrine now differ from that preached by Mr. Wesley at Oxford?

Answer. Chiefly in these two points; first, he then knew nothing of that righteousness of faith in justification; nor second, of that nature of faith itself, as implying consciousness of pardon.

Question 23. May not some degree of the love of God go before a distinct sense of justification? *Answer.* We believe it may.

Question 24. Can any degree of holiness or sanctification?

Answer. Many degrees of outward holiness may; yea, and some degrees of meekness, and several other tempters which would be branches of Christian holiness, but that they do not spring from Christian principles. For the abiding love of God cannot spring but from a faith in a pardoning God. And no true Christian holiness can exist without that love of God for its foundation.

Question 25. Is every man as soon as he believes a new creature, sanctified, pure in heart? Has he then a new heart? Does Christ dwell therein? And is he a temple of the Holy Ghost?

Answer. All these things may be affirmed of every believer in a true sense. Let us not, therefore, contradict those who maintain it. Why should we contend about words?

Sin

May none of us be like Ahab, to rob our brother of their vineyard (1 Kings 21:14-20). Be sure your sin will find you out (Numbers 32:23). Judas' sin found him. Cain's sin found him. *

---

*This short section was at the end of the index. It had no heading. This could be a veiled reference to the several antagonists who had tried to take the mission from Seymour over the years. *Ed.*

Speaking in Tongues

When we set up tongues to be the Bible evidence of baptism in the Holy Ghost and fire only, we have left the divine word of God and have instituted our own teaching. But if we will take the divine word of God, it will lead us right. Ezekiel 14, says when a man set up any idols in his heart and seek the Lord, and if the prophet be deceived. He says he is the one that deceives the prophet (Ezekiel 14:9).

While tongues is one of the signs that follows God's Spirit-filled children, they will have to know the truth and do the truth. If not, grievous wolves will enter in among the flock and tear asunder the sheep. How will they get in? They will come in through the sign gift of speaking in tongues, and if God's children did not know anything more than that to be the evidence, they would not have a hard time entering in among them and scatter them. The Holy Ghost gives men and women wisdom to execute the power of His word (1 Cor. 4:20).*

The Gift of Tongues

How do we take the gift of tongues? We believe that all God's children that have faith in God can pray to God for an outpouring of the Holy Spirit upon the holy sanctified life and receive a great filling of the Holy Spirit and speak in new tongues, as the Spirit gives utterance. But we don't base our faith on it as essential to our salvation. Some one will ask, How do you know when you will get the Holy Ghost? He, the Spirit of Truth, will guide you into all truth (St. John 16:13). The gift of the

*In the original, this section on speaking in tongues was under the heading, "The Plan of Salvation." *Ed.*

Holy Ghost is more than speaking in the tongues. He is wisdom, power, truth, holiness. He is a person that teaches us the truth.

How does our doctrine differ with the other Pentecostal brethren? First, they claim that a man or woman has not the Holy Spirit, except they speak in tongues. So that is contrary to the teaching of Christ. Matt. 7:21-23. If we would base our faith on tongues being the evidence of the gift of the Holy Ghost, it would knock out our faith in the blood of Christ and the inward witness of the Holy Spirit bearing witness with our spirit (Rom. 8:14-16).*

---

*In the original, this section on speaking in tongues was under the heading, "The Support of the Ministry." Seymour's views on speaking in tongues could be very controversial. Some classical Pentecostals may argue that he denied an essential element of the faith, that tongues are the initial, physical evidence of the Holy Spirit baptism. Others who have argued against the classical position will use Seymour's words to vindicate their position. In the editor's opinion, both will be taking Seymour's words to an extreme he did not intend.

First, let me say that Seymour was a pastor and not a theologian. He had very little education and had some difficulty expressing himself clearly. Careful study would indicate that Seymour's main concern is that speaking in tongues is not seen as the *only* evidence of the Holy Spirit baptism or as an essential to salvation.

Seymour's early position on tongues was recorded regularly in *The Apostolic Faith,* the official organ of the Azusa Street Mission, "The baptism with the Holy Ghost is a gift of power upon the sanctified life; so when we get it we have the same evidence as the disciples received on the day of Pentecost (Acts 2:3, 40, in speaking in new tongues.*"*

It is possible that Seymour is reevaluating his position on tongues because so many "tongue speaking" Christians that he had dealt with over the years had shown such little evidence of a Holy Ghost baptized life. Charles Parham, William Durham and a number of other Pentecostal leaders had caused Seymour much grief and split the Azusa congregation on multiple occasions. *Ed.*

Qualifications and Work

No one in our church shall be known as a preacher because he or she speaks in tongues; no one in our work shall be known as receiving the Holy Ghost simply because he or she speaks in tongues alone (1 Corinthians 13).

The Nature of Man in His Present State

I. When God created man
   1. He made him but a little lower than the angels (Psalms 8:4-7)
   2. He made him in His Own image and exact likeness (Gen. 1:26, 27)
      (a). God is a Spirit (John 4:24)
      (b). A spirit hath not flesh and bones (Luke 24:39)
      (c). God is invisible (Col. 1:15; 1 Tim. 1:17; Heb. 11:27)
      (d). God is immortal (1 Tim. 1:17)
      (e). To create man in God's likeness and image would be to create him a spirit being, immortal, and immaterial (Job 32:8; Eccl. 12:7)
   3. He formed a spirit in man (Zech. 12:1)

The State of Man between Death and the Judgment

I. Natural death
   1. Separates the soul from the body (Gen. 35:18; Luke 12:20)
   2. Is the time when the soul leaves the body (Gen. 35:18)

3. Does not involve the soul in its ruin (2 Cor. 4:16; Matt. 10:28)

II. At natural death.
   1. The body returns to dust (Gen. 3:19; Psalm 104:29; Eccl. 12:7)
      (a). It sleeps (Dan. 12:2; Matt. 7:52)
      (b). It knows nothing (Eccl. 9:5, 6)
   2. The spirit goes to God (Eccl. 12:7; Act 7:59; Luke 23:46)

III. The state of the soul after death.
   1. The righteous are in a heavenly realm called Paradise.

The Future State

I. Man will not receive his full reward and punishment until after the resurrection, beyond the judgment (2 Tim. 4:1,8; Eccl. 12:14; Rev. 20:11-15; 2 Cor. 5:10; Rom. 14:10-12; 2 Pet. 2:9; Matt. 16:26; 2 Thess. 1:7-10; Matt. 25:31-46)
II. The reward of the righteous
   1. Will be in heaven (Matt. 5:11,12; Matt. 6:19, 20; Matt. 19:21; Luke 6:22, 23)
   2. Heaven will be our future and eternal home (Heb. 10:34; 1 Pet. 1:4,5; Col. 1:5; 2 Tim. 4:18)
   3. Heaven is a prepared place (John 14:2, 3; 2 Cor. 5:1)
      (a). Like the "Lamb slain from the foundation of the world," heaven was prepared in the mind of God, in His divine plan, from the beginning (Rev. 13:8; Matt. 25:34).
      (b). Christ in reality had to be slain, also went and really prepared our future place of abode (John 14:2, 3; Rev. 7:9-17)

4. Heaven is termed
   (a). A city (Heb. 13:14; Rev. 22:14)
   (b). A country (Heb. 11:16)
   (c). New heavens and new earth (2 Pet. 3:7-13; Rev. 20:11-15; Rev. 21:1)

III. The punishment of the wicked
  1. The future punishment of the wicked will be in hell, which is a place prepared for the everlasting punishment of demons (Matt. 25:41; 2 Pet. 2:4, 5; Jude 6)
   (a). Hell is a place (Luke 12:4,5)
   (b). Hell is a place prepared (Matt. 25:41)
   (c). The wicked shall be turned into hell (Psalm 9:17)
  2. The place and state of future punishment is termed outer darkness, and in that darkness the wicked shall weep, wail, and gnash their teeth forever
   (a). Outer darkness (Matt. 8:11,12; Matt. 25:30)
   (b). There shall be wailing and gnashing of teeth (Matt. 24:50, 51)
   (c). The wicked shall remain there forever (2 Peter 2:9, 13-17; Jude 13)
  3. The place and state of future punishment is termed a lake of fire, which will be everlasting fire, and in this everlasting fire the wicked will suffer an everlasting punishment.
   (a). A lake of fire (Rev. 20:15; Rev. 21:8)
   (b). Hell fire (Matt. 18:19; Mark 9:47)
   (c). Fire that never shall be quenched (Mark 9:43-48)
   (d). Everlasting fire (Matt. 18:8; Matt. 25:41)
   (e). Suffering the vengeance of eternal fire (Jude 7)

(f). Everlasting punishment (Matt. 25:46; Rev. 20:10)

4. The future punishment of the wicked consists in torment and that torment will last forever and ever

(a). Torment (Matt. 8:28, 29; Rev. 14:10)

(b). Forever and ever (Rev. 14:10,11; Rev. 20:10)

5. The future punishment of the wicked consists in damnation.

The Saved Souls Are at Rest
Luke 23:43

I. Abraham's bosom (Luke 16:22)

1. Are dwelling with Christ (Phil. 1:21-24)
2. Are absent from the body and present with the Lord (2 Cor. 5:19)
3. Are dwelling with their people (Gen. 49:33; Gen. 50:1-13)
4. Are in a state of blessedness (Rev. 14:13)
5. Are at rest (Job 3:17)
6. Are comforted (Luke 16:25)
7. Are conscious (1 Thes. 5:10; Rev. 6:9,10; Luke 16:22, 25, 26)

II. The wicked

1. Are in conscious suffering (Luke 16:22-24)
2. Are reserved in chains of darkness unto the judgment day, when they will be punished

Annihilate

To reduce to nothing or non-existence; to destroy the existence of; to cause to cease to be.

We don't believe in the doctrine of the annihilation of the wicked. That is the reason why we could not stand for tongues being the evidence of the baptism in the Holy Ghost and fire. If tongues were the evidence of the gift of the Holy Spirit, then men and women that have received the gift of tongues could not believe contrary to the teachings of the Holy Spirit. Since tongues are not the evidence of the baptism in the Holy Spirit, men and women can receive it (tongues) and yet be destitute of the truth. It's one of the signs, not the evidence (Mark 16:16-18). The Holy Spirit came from heaven to guide us in to all truth. So annihilation of the soul is not the Holy Spirit's, nor Jesus' teaching, for both the Holy Spirit's and Jesus' teaching are all the same. Annihilation of the wicked, or the annihilation of a soul is contrary to scripture (Matt. 10:28). Jesus said in Matt. 10:28: "And fear not them which kill the body, but are not able to kill the soul." Jesus showed that our soul or inner spirit is immortal (Matt. 10:28; Rev. 6:9-11; 1 Pet. 3:3-4). Annihilation means to reduce to nothing or nonexistence; to destroy the existence of; to cause to cease to be. If a man's soul was not immortal, he would be no higher that the beast or the apes and monkeys, but not so. Our bodies are the only thing that is mortal. *

---

*Charles F. Parham, who many hold to be the father of modern Pentecostalism, taught this strange doctrine of the annihilation of the wicked. Seymour was a student in Parham's classes in Houston before going to California and pastoring the Azusa Street Mission. It is clear that he felt a responsibility to take special care in repudiating this doctrinal error. *Ed.*

The doctrine of materialism was advocated by the ancient sect of the Sadducees (Acts 23:8). The Sadducees were a sect that did not believe in the doctrine of the resurrection of the dead; they did not believe in angels or spirits. But, the Pharisees confessed both (Acts. 23:8). Now, many people of today that deny the immortality of the soul are nothing but modern Sadducees, saying man's soul is just his breath. Man has a spirit. God only hath immortality (1Tim. 6:15-16).

Materialism is the doctrine that denies the immortality of the soul. They maintain that the soul of man is not a spirit substance distinct from matter.

I. God only hath immortality (1Tim. 6:15,16)
    1. This text has direct reference to Jesus Christ and not to the Father (1 Tim. 6:14-16)
    2. Jesus Christ is King of Kings and Lord of Lords (Rev. 17:14; Rev.19:16)
    3. To take this text in an exclusive unqualified sense would deny the immortality of the Father and of angels (Matt. 22:29, 30)
    4. We yet inhabit mortal flesh, mortal bodies, which are subject to physical death; while Christ has already received His immortal, resurrected body, and death hath no dominion over Him. In this sense He only hath attained immortality (Rom. 6:9)
    5. This text referring to the resurrection of these bodies has not a feather's weight of evidence against the immortality of the soul

II. Seek for immortality (Rom. 2:7)
    1. We are mortal in body (Rom. 6:12: 2 Cor. 4:11)
    2. Our soul or spirit is immortal (Matt. 10:28; Rev. 6:9-11; 1 Pet. 3:3, 4)

3. Our bodies are the only part of us that will put on immortality in the resurrection (Phil. 3:20,21; 1 Cor. 15:42-44)
4. To seek for immortality is to so live that we may have a glorious resurrection in an immortal and glorified body to eternal rewards in heaven. Again, this proves nothing against the immortality of the soul (1 Cor. 15:51-53)

III. The dead know not anything (Eccl. 9:5, 6)
1. This applies to the outer man–the body–that part of us which returns to dust (Gen. 3:19; Psalm 104:29; Dan.12:2)
2. It cannot apply to the real inner man, the soul, for that remains conscious after death (Luke 16:19-31; 1 Cor. 5:1-9; 1 Thess. 5:10; Rev. 6:9,10)

IV. In the day of death our thoughts perish (Psalm 146:4)
1. The mind is one thing, and its thoughts, schemes, purposes, and intentions, quite another (Isa. 59:7; Jer. 4:14; Mark 7:21)
2. While the schemes, plans, and thoughts of worldly hearts are cut off by death, and perish, the heart lives forever (Psalm 146:4; Psalm 22:26)

V. Against eternal punishment
1. The wages of sin is death (Rom. 6:22; Ezek. 18:4)
   (a). Sin produces death to the soul the very day that man transgresses God's law (Gen. 2:17; Rom. 7:9)
   (b). Sin separates from God now (Isa. 59:1)
   (c). All sinners are now dead, yet have a conscious existence (Eph. 2:1; Rom. 8:6; 1 John 3:14; 1 Tim. 5:6)

(d). These scriptures plainly show that the death of the soul is incurred by sin and is not the destruction of its consciousness. The sinner still lives. It is the forfeiture of the bliss of divine favor. Not a cessation of conscious existence, but an alienation from God, whose favor is the normal sphere of the soul's happiness. Sinners are now dead, yet live. They are cut off from God's favor. Just so in the future, they will be cut off from union with God eternally. Dead, yet they have a conscious existence and will be tormented forever and ever in the lake of fire, which is the second death (Rev. 21:28; Rev. 20:10).

2. Eternal life is only promised to the righteous through Jesus Christ (Rom 6:22)

(a). Eternal life is not only eternal conscious existence, but a blessed union with God, enjoyment in His service and favor without end. A blessed knowledge of His salvation (John 17:3)

(b). Eternal life given by the word and Spirit of God reunites the soul to God and makes it alive to His glory. This blessed life is now attainable in this life (Eph. 2:1, 5, 6; 1 John 3:14; John 5:24; John 6:47; 1 John 6:47; 1 John 5:11,13)

(c). If we prove faithful until death, the same blessed union with God and eternal life we here enjoy in the world to come (Mark 10:30)

(d). At the second coming of Christ, death, will be destroyed, the righteous will be raised to eternal life, and the wicked to shame and everlasting contempt (1 Cor. 15:22-26; John 5:28,29; Dan. 12:2)

3. The wicked shall be destroyed (2 Thes. 1:7-10; Psalm 37:38)

(a). Destroy does not always necessarily mean to annihilate. It also means to ruin, to render utterly useless for the purpose for which it was made. Floods may destroy cities and not annihilate them. Storms may destroy crops and not annihilate them.

(b). Examples of its use in the scripture

(1). Israel destroyed herself, but was not blotted out of existence as a nation (Hos. 13:9)

(2). A hypocrite with his mouth destroyeth his neighbor, but does not annihilate him (Prov. 11:9)

(3). We may destroy our brother by eating meat, yet he will have a living existence (Rom. 14:15)

(4). Destroy—to trouble (Psalm 78:45)

(5). Destroy—to pervert (Eccl. 7:7)

(6). Paul destroyed God's people by putting them in prison. They were not annihilated (Acts 9:21; Acts 8:3)

(7). Faith was destroyed, yet lived (Gal. 1:23)

(8). Moral destruction, but conscious existence (2 Chr. 26:16)

(9). Destroy—to spoil (Jer. 4:20)

(c). From all these scripture texts we learn that destroy does not imply annihilation. So with the destruction of the wicked. It will not be a blotting out of existence as the heathen vainly hope; but an eternal separation from God, a deprivation of his approving smile and favor. Since man was created to enjoy God,

love and serve Him, when eternally disquali-
fied by sin for that lofty end, he is ruined,
destroyed, from the fact that he will never
answer the exalted object of his creation.
Being still conscious he will suffer an end-
less punishment (Rev. 20:10).

4. The wicked shall perish (Luke 13:1-5)
   (a). The word perish does not imply annihilation
   for the following reasons:
   (1). The righteous perish as well as the
   wicked (Eccl. 7:15; Isa. 57:1; Mich. 7:2)
   (2). Truth may perish, but still live (Jer. 7:28)
   (b). The sense in which the wicked shall perish
   is that their doom is unredeemable, and eternal, and there will be no hope of recovery
   from the state of torment.

The Church

The Character of the Church

A church constitutes a kind of spiritual kingdom in the world, but not of the world; whose king is Christ; whose law is His word; whose institutions are His ordinances; whose duty is His service; whose reward is His blessing.

In all matters of faith and conscience, as well as in all matters of internal order and government, a church is "under law to Christ;" (1 Cor. 9:21) but as men and citizens, its members must "submit themselves to governors," (1 Peter 2:14) like other men, so far as shall not interfere with, or contravene, the claims of the divine law and authority upon them. They must "render unto Caesar the things that are Caesar's, and unto God the things that are God's" remembering that God's claims are supreme, and annihilate all claims that contradict or oppose them (Matt. 22:21).

The Design of Church

The evident design of our Saviour in founding and preserving the church in the world, was, that it should be a monument in the midst of guilty men, bearing perpetual witness against the wickedness of the world, and to the goodness of God. But especially that she should be living testimonies to the work of redemption, "the light of the world," and "the salt of the earth" (Matt. 5:13,14).

The church constitutes the effective instrumentality by which the will of God and the knowledge of salvation through Christ are made known to men; at the same time she forms homes for the saints on earth; sheep-folds for the safety of the flock, and schools for the instruction and training of the children of the covenant; while she encourages the penitent and warns the careless. The church should well understand her "high calling," and seek to accomplish it, according to the will of God" (Gal. 1:4).

The Authority of the Church

The authority of a church is limited to its own members, and applies to all matters of Christian character, and whatever involves the welfare of religion. It is designed to secure in all its members a conduct and conversation "becoming godliness."

This authority is derived directly from God; not from states nor princes, nor people; not from its own officers, nor its members, nor from any other source of ecclesiastical or civil power or right. But Christ "is head over all things to the church" and also as of right, "the church is subject to Christ" (Eph. 1:22; Eph. 5:24).

The Church and its Mission

The mission of the Church is to "Go ye therefore and teach all nations, baptizing them in the name of the Father, and of the Son, and the Holy Ghost. Teaching them to observe all things whatsoever I have commanded you; and lo, I am with you always, even unto the end of the world. Amen." Now, the church is to teach all that the Saviour commanded it to teach (Matt. 28:19-20; Matt. 10:1-14; Luke 9:1-6; Luke 10:1-20; Luke 22:35-37).

So the church is to hold fast to Christ's teaching until He comes. Our children are to be instructed in their homes; the little babes are to be blessed by the church. Christ commanded to bring the little children to the church and have them blessed. "And they brought young children to Him, that He should touch them; and his disciples rebuked those that brought them. But when Jesus saw it, He was much displeased, and said unto them, Suffer the little children to come unto me, and forbid them not: for of such is the kingdom of God. Verily I say unto you, Whosoever shall not receive the kingdom of God as a little child, he shall not enter therein. And He took them up in His arms, put His hands upon them, and blessed them" (Mark 10:13-16).

Church Membership

The character of a building depends very much on the materials of which it is constructed. Christian disciples "are builded together for a habitation of God, through the Spirit" (Eph. 2:21-22; 1 Peter 2:1-15).

Some times the material of the church is in such a shape until it limits God in His great salvation. In order for a church to prosper, she must obey Jesus' teaching in all things. Jesus can not put his approval on a church that won't obey His teachings. In the book of Revelation, the church had backslid so far from Jesus' teaching until we find Him knocking at the door for admittance, so when a church has backslidden so far from God it can not demand anything from God until it repent from its sin (**Rev. 2:1-8**).

The proper material for the character of the church, is men and women saved from sin, who hate sin, and live free from fornication and adultery and all uncleanness. And, who have faith in God's word, believing for the faith that was once delivered to the Saints (Acts 15:29; Jude 1-3).

The church would have to believe in healing the sick, casting out demons and believe in all the signs following the church, which Christ said would follow (Acts 2:1-4; Acts 4:29-31).

Our colored brethren must love our white brethren and respect them in the truth so that the word of God can have its free course, and our white brethren must love their colored brethren and respect them in the truth so that the Holy Spirit won't be grieved. I hope we won't have any more trouble and division spirit.*

Membership: Reception on Probation

No one to be taken on probation except he is born of God or on watch care; except he or she knows the Lord, in order to prevent improper persons from gaining admission into the church of Jesus Christ, and in order to the exercise of the power of godly admonition and discipline (Matt.16:13-18; Acts 5:1-11; Acts 8:18-24).

1. Let great care be taken in receiving persons on probation and let no one be enrolled as a watchcare member unless he give satisfactory evidence of an earnest desire to be saved from all sin and enjoy the

---

*The foundation for this section is borrowed from *Principles and Practices for Baptist Churches*. Obviously, most of the material is original, including Seymour's notes on division among blacks and whites. The pain he has suffered from racism is evident in these words. *Ed.*

fellowship of God's people. Let the pastor and the deacons and elders see that all persons on probation be early made acquainted with the doctrine, and rules and regulations of the Apostolic Faith Church.

2. Probationers are expected to conform carefully to all the rules and usages of the church. They are entitled to all its spiritual privileges and aids; but they may not be members in full until they have proven themselves to be true in every way.

Admission into Full Membership

1. Let no one be admitted into full membership in the church until he has been at least six months on probation, has been recommended by the leaders and elders meeting, or born of the Spirit and baptized, and on examination by the pastor before the church has given satisfactory assurances both of the correctness of his faith and of his willingness to observe and keep the rules of the church.

2. Nevertheless, a member in good standing in an orthodox Evangelical church desiring to unite with us may, on giving satisfactory answers to the unusual inquiries, be received at once into full membership, if they have been born of the spirit and believe our doctrine.

3. Let the pastor and the committee on church records be careful to see that the names of all persons received into the church are duly recorded, and the pastor shall report at each monthly meeting all changes that have occurred in the membership during the monthly meeting.

The Trial of an Accused Member

Immoral Conduct

A member of the church accused of immorality shall be brought to trial before a committee of not less than five members of the church who are in good standing. They shall be chosen by the preacher in charge, and, if he judge it to be necessary, he may select them and the parties may challenge for cause. The preacher in charge shall preside in the trial, and shall cause a correct record of the proceedings and evidence to be made.

If the accused person be found guilty by the decision of a majority of the committee and the crime be such as is expressly forbidden in the word of God, sufficient to exclude a person from the kingdom of grace and glory, let the preacher in charge expel him.

But if in view of mitigating circumstances and of humble and penitent confession the committee find that a lower penalty is proper, it may either impose censure on the offender, or suspend him from all church privileges for a definite time, at its discretion.

Imprudent and Unchristian Conduct

In cases of neglect of duties of any kind, imprudent conduct, indulging in sinful tempers or words, the buying, selling or using intoxicating liquors as a beverage, signing petitions in favor of granting a license for the sale of intoxicating liquors, becoming bondsmen for persons engaged in such traffic, renting property as a place in or on which to manufacture or sell intoxicating liquors, dancing, playing at games of chance, attending theaters, horse races, circuses, dancing parties, or patronizing dancing schools, or taking such other amusements as are obviously of misleading or questionable moral tendency, or disobedience to the order and discipline of the church:*

On the first offense, let private reproof be given by the pastor or leader, and if there be an acknowledgment of the fault, and proper humiliation, the person may be borne with.

On the second offense the pastor or leader may take one or two discreet members of the church.

On a third offense let him be brought to trial, and if found guilty, and there be no sign of real humiliation, he shall be expelled.

Neglect of the Means of Grace

When a member of our church habitually neglects the means of grace, such as the public worship of God, the supper of the Lord, family and private prayer, searching the scriptures, praise meetings and prayer meetings:

First, let the preacher in charge, whenever it is practicable, visit him and explain to him the consequence if he continue to neglect.

Second, if he does not amend, let the preacher in charge bring his case before a committee of not less than five who are members in good standing before which he shall be cited to appear. And if he be found guilty of willful neglect by the decision of a majority of the members before whom the case is brought, let him be excluded.

Disobedient members have ruled the preacher in this church before (Titus 1:5-14; 1 Thess. 5:12-23).

---

*If Pentecostal churches today held to this same standard of conduct for membership, most of the church rolls would be blank. *Ed.*

Causing Dissension

If a member of our church shall be accused of endeavoring to sow dissension in any of our churches by inveighing against either our doctrines or discipline, the person so offending shall first be reproved by the preacher in charge; and if he persist in such pernicious practice, he shall be brought to trial, and, if found guilty, shall be expelled.

Disagreement in Business; Arbitration

On any disagreement between two or more members of our church concerning business transactions which cannot be settled by the parties, the preacher in charge shall inquire into the circumstances of the case, and shall recommend to the parties a reference, consisting of two arbiters chosen by one party, and two chosen by the other party, which four arbiters so chosen shall choose a fifth; the five arbiters being members of our church. The preacher in charge shall preside, and the disciplinary forms of trial shall be observed.

If either party refuse to abide by the judgment of the arbiters, he shall be brought to trial, and if he fail to show sufficient cause for refusal, he shall be expelled.

If, in the case of debt or dispute, one of the parties is a minister, one of the duties laid on the preacher in charge in the foregoing paragraph shall be performed by the presiding elder of the minister concerned. If both are ministers, the presiding elder of either may act in the case.

Insolvency

The preachers in charge are required to execute all our rules fully and strenuously against all frauds and particularly against dishonest insolvency, suffering none to remain in our church, on any account, who are found guilty of any fraud.

To prevent scandal, when any member of the church fails in business, or contracts debts which he is not able to pay, let two or three judicious members of the church inspect the accounts, contracts and circumstances of the supposed delinquent; and if they judge that he has behaved dishonestly or borrowed money without a probability of paying, let him be brought to trial, and, if found guilty, expelled.

General Directions Concerning Trials

In all cases of trial of members let all witnesses for the church be duly notified by the preacher in charge. The order concerning absent witnesses and witnesses from without shall be the same as that observed in the trial of ministers. The accused shall have the right to call to his assistance as counsel any member or minister in good and regular standing in the Apostolic Faith Church.

The Necessity of Union among Ourselves

Let us be deeply sensible (from what we have known) of the evil of a division in principle, spirit or practice, and the dreadful consequences to ourselves and others. If we are united, what can stand before us? If we divide, we shall destroy ourselves, and the work of God, and the souls of our people (Gal. 5:15-17). In order to have a closer union with each other:
1. Let us be deeply convinced of the absolute necessity of it.
2. Pray earnestly for and speak freely to each other.
3. When we meet let us never part without prayer.
4. Take great care not to despise each other's gifts.

5. Never speak lightly of each other.

6. Let us defend each other's character in everything so far as is consistent with truth.

7. Labor in honor each to prefer the other before himself. We recommend a serious perusal of the causes, evils and cures of heart and church divisions.

Deportment at the Conference or Convention

It is desired that all things be considered on these occasions as in the immediate presence of God. That every person speak freely whatever is in his heart.

In order, therefore, that we may best improve our time at the convention:

1. While we are conversing let us have an especial care to set God always before us.

2. In the intermediate hours let us redeem all the time we can for private exercise.

3. There, let us give ourselves to prayer for one another, and for a blessing on our labor.

The Ministry

The Call to Preach

In order that we may try those persons who profess to be moved by the Holy Ghost to preach, let the following questions be asked, namely:

1. Do they know God as a pardoning God? Have they the love of God abiding in them? Do they desire nothing but God? Are they holy in all manner of conversation? Have they been sanctified wholly unto God? (John 17:15-17; 1 Thess. 4 and 3, 5, 22-24; Acts 2-4; Acts 19:6).

2. Have they gifts, as well as grace, for the work? Have they, in some tolerable degree, a clear, sound understanding; a right judgment in the things of God; a just conception of salvation by faith? Has God given them any degree of utterance? Do they speak justly, readily, clearly? Have they been annointed by the Holy Ghost? Have any been truly convinced of sin and converted to God under their preaching? Have any been sanctified and healed and baptized in the Holy Ghost through their preaching? And are believers edified by their preaching?

3. As long as these marks concur in any one we believe he is called by God to preach. These we receive as sufficient proof that he is moved by the Holy Ghost.

Rules For a Preacher's Conduct

1. Be diligent. Never unemployed. Never be triflingly employed. Never trifle away time. Neither spend any more time at any place than is strictly necessary.

2. Be serious. Let your motto be "Holiness to the Lord." Avoid all lightness, jesting and foolish talking.

3. Converse sparingly, and conduct yourself prudently with women (1 Tim. 5:2).

4. Believe evil of no one without good evidence; unless you see it done take heed how you credit it. Put the best construction on everything. You know the judge is always supposed to be on the prisoner's side.

5. Speak evil of no one, because your word especially, would eat as a doth a canker. Keep your thoughts within your own breast till you come to the person concerned.

6. Tell every one under your care what you think wrong in his conduct and temper, and that lovingly and plainly, as soon as may be; else it will fester in your heart. Make all haste to cast the fire out of your bosom.

7. Avoid all affectation. A preacher of the gospel is the servant of all.

8. Be ashamed of nothing but sin.

9. Be punctual. Do everything exactly at the time. And, do not mend our rules, but keep them; not for wrath but for conscience' sake.

10. You have nothing to do but to save souls; therefore spend and be spent in this work; and go always not only to those that want you, but those that want you most.

Observe! It is not your business only to preach so many times and to take care of this or that Mission but to save as many as you can; to bring as many sinners as you can to repentance, and with all your power to build them up in that holiness without which they cannot see the Lord. And remember, an Apostlic Faith preacher is to mind every point, great and small, in the discipline. Therefore, you will need to exercise all the wisdom and grace you have.

11. Act in all things not according to your own will, but as a son in the gospel. As such, it is your duty to employ your time in the manner in which we direct; in preaching and visiting from house to house; in reading, meditation and prayer. Above all, if you labor with us in the Lord's vineyard, it is needful you should do that part of the work which we advise, at those times and places which we judge most for his glory.

Smaller advices which might be of use to us are perhaps these:

1. Be sure never to disappoint a congregation.

2. Begin at the time appointed.

3. Let your whole deportment be serious, weighty and solemn.

Duties of a Preacher

The duties of a preacher are:

1. To preach.

2. To meet the members of the church.

3. To visit the sick.*

---

*This section was under "Spiritual Qualifications" in the original. *Ed.*

Rules for the Ministry

The discipline of the Azusa Street Apostolic Faith Mission is the New Testament which is the perfect law of government.

1. We must have government in all things (2 Tim. 3:17; Psalm 119:142; John 1:17; Gal. 6:2).

2. The Bible teaches the qualification of the ministry (Luke 24:49; Acts 1:5, 8; Acts 2:4; Titus 1:9,11; 2 Cor. 3:6).

3. It teaches the character of a true minister (1 Tim. 3:1-7; 1 Tim. 4:2; Titus 2:7, 8).

4. It teaches the duties of a true minister (Acts 20:28; John 21:15).

5. It gives the circuit for the ministry (Matt. 28:19; Mark 16:15, 16).

6. It gives instructions as to their ordination (Acts 13:2, 4; Titus 1:4, 9).

7. It gives instructions how to proceed in case a ministry goes astray (Gal. 6:1, 2; 2 Thes. 3:15; 2 Tim. 2:24, 26; 1 Tim. 5:19, 20; 2 Thes. 3:16).

8. It teaches how to deal with the members. It teaches their duty to each other (James 4:11; Col. 3:16; 1 Peter 1:22; 1 Thes. 5:11, 14, 15; Matt. 14:15; Heb. 3:1).

9. It teaches them how to proceed in case of trespass (Luke 18:3, 5; Matt. 18:15, 18; Col. 3:12, 14; Eph. 4:31, 32).

10. A discipline that contains more than the New Testament is faulty, and it contains too much; if less than the New Testament it is faulty; it contains too little (Deut. 4:2; Prov. 30:5, 6; Rev. 22:18).

Christ governs His church which He purchased with His own blood, through His word by the operation of the Spirit.

Spiritual Qualification

A preacher should be qualified for his charge by walking closely with God and having his work greatly at heart and by understanding and loving discipline, ours in particular.

We do not sufficiently watch over each other. Should we not frequently ask each other: Do you walk closely with God? Have you now fellowship with the Father and the Son? Do you spend the day in the manner with which the Lord would be pleased? Do you converse seriously, usefully and closely? To be made particular: Do you use all the means of grace yourself and enforce the use of them on all other persons?

The means of grace are either instituted or prudential.

Instituted means of grace are:

1. Prayer: private, family and public, consisting of deprecation, pretition, intercession and thanksgiving. Do you use each of these? Do you forecast daily, wherever you are, to secure time for private devotion? Do you practice it everywhere? Do you ask everywhere: Have you family prayer? Do you ask individuals? Do you use private prayer every morning and evening in particular?

2. Searching the scriptures. First: Reading; constantly some part of every day; regularly, all the Bible in order; carefully, with prayer; seriously, with prayer before and after; fruitfully, immediately practicing what you learn there. Second: Meditating; at set times; by rule. Third; Hearing, at every opportunity, with prayer before, at, after. Have you a Bible always about you?

3. Footwashing. Do you use this ordinance at every opportunity?

4. The Lord's Supper. Do you use this at every opportunity? With solemn prayer before? With earnest and deliberate self-devotion?

5. Fasting. Do you use as much abstinence and fasting every week as your health, strength, and labor will permit?

6. Christian Conference. Are you convinced how important and how difficult it is to order your conversation aright? Is it always in grace? Seasoned with salt? Meet to minister grace to the hearers? Do you not converse too long at a time? Is not an hour commonly enough? Would it not be well always to have a determined end in view? And to pray before and after it?

Prudential means of grace we may use either as Christians as apostles or as preachers.*

1. As Christians: What particular rules have you in order to grow in grace? What arts of holy living?

2. As apostolic: Do you ever miss your prayer meeting?

3. As Apostolics: Have you thoroughly considered your duty, and do you make a conscience of executing every part of it? Do you meet every meeting and the leaders?

These means may be used without fruit. But there are some means which cannot, namely: watching, denying ourselves, taking up our cross, exercise of the presence of God.

---

*Wesley's questions were for "Common Christians, Methodists, Preachers and Assistants. Seymour adapted to the Apostolic Faith. *Ed.*

4. Do you steadily watch against the world? Yourself? Your besetting sin? (Heb. 12:1-2).

And we are not more knowing because we are idle. We forget our first rule. "Be diligent." Never be unemployed. Never be triflingly employed. Neither spend any more time at any place than is strictly necessary. We fear there is altogether a fault in this mater, and that few of us are clear. Which of us spend as many hours a day in God's work as we did formerly in man's work. We talk or read what comes next to hand. We must, absolutely must, cure this evil, or betray the cause of God. But how? First, read the most useful books and that regularly and constantly.

Where and How to Preach

It is by no means advisable for us to preach in as many places as we can without forming any mission. We have made the trial in various places, and that for a considerable time. But all that seed has fallen by the wayside. There is scarcely any fruit remaining.

We should endeavor to preach most:

1. Where there is the greatest number of quiet and willing hearers.

2. Where there is most fruit. Let us walk so close to God that His Spirit will direct us (Acts 8:26, 39).

We ought diligently to observe in what places God is pleased at any time to pour out His Spirit more abundantly, and at that time to send more laborers than usual into that part of the harvest.

The best general method of preaching is:

1. To convince.

2. To offer Christ.

3. To invite.

4. To build up. And to do this in some measure in every sermon.

The most effectual way of preaching Christ is to preach Him in all His offices, and to declare His law, as well as His gospel, both to believers and unbelievers. Let us strongly and closely insist upon inward and outward holiness in all its branches.

The Support of the Ministry

Our ministers that labor in the work of the Lord and give all their time to the gospel should be supported by the gospel (1 Tim. 5:17-18). Those that labor in doctrine and giving the word should be nicely carried, for they are worthy of it (1 Cor. 9:7-11). We must support the gospel or the gospel will die on our hands and the enemy will get in and destroy the flock of God.

Women in the Ministry

All ordination must be done by men not women. Women may be ministers but not to baptize and ordain in this work.*

---

*In the original, this section on women in ministry was under the heading, "The Plan of Salvation." *Ed.*

William J. Seymour at the Mission
Photo Used by Permission
Flower Pentecostal Heritage Center

William J. and Jennie Evans Moore Seymour
Photo used by permission
Flower Pentecostal Heritage Center

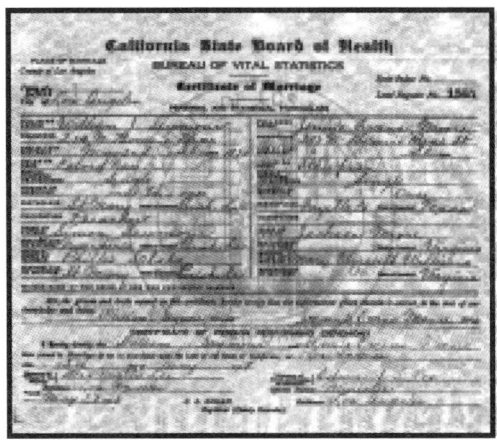

Moore and Seymour Marriage License

Marriage and the Family

A Christian Home

A Christian home is one of the sweetest places on God's green earth. It is a place where God is honored. A place where the Christ of God is worshipped! O how blessed it is to enter a Christian home where God is honored! God is mindful of our homes for we read in Gen. 18:17, 19. God said, "Shall I hide from Abraham the destruction of Sodom and Gomorrah? Shall I hide from Abraham that thing which I do, seeing that Abraham shall surely become a great nation and all the nations of the earth shall be blessed in him: for I know him." Praise the Lord! God knows us. He knows our hearts, praise His name!

Just listen to what God said about Abraham? Can he say that about every home? This is a standard for us to go by. I know him that he will command his children and his household. Everything followed him. That is to say that the whole family would follow the example of Abraham in holiness and obedience to God's word. It is so blessed when you can find a home saved.

The father takes his place at the head of the home (Eph. 5:23). He rules it according to the word of God. Again God says, "And they shall keep the way of the Lord to do justice and judgment: that the Lord may bring upon Abraham that which He has spoken of him.

To be a bishop a man must have a home that will measure up to the word, he must be one that ruleth well his own house, having his children in subjection with all gravity, for if a man know not how to rule his own house how shall he take care of the Church of God (1 Tim. 3:4, 5).

We read again in the Old Testament from Joshua 24:15, 16. Joshua could speak for his whole family. When the Israelites were going astray after other gods, Joshua brought them together and said, "If it seem evil unto you to serve the Lord, choose you this day whom you will serve; whether the gods which your fathers serve that were on the other side of the flood, or the gods of the Amorites in whose land ye dwell: but as for me and my house, we will serve the Lord. And the people answered and said, "God forbid that we should forsake the Lord, to serve other gods." We can see that Joshua's home was a home for God. The promise is to you and your children (Acts 2:39).

We see in another place in the word where God saved a whole home in one night. The Philippian jailer was saved and his whole household (Acts 16:32). This was a wonderful time in the prison. O how sweet it is to be a servant of God! We see that they had been beaten for this gospel. But they were not discouraged. They prayed and sang at midnight and heaven and earth met together in that jail and God shook all the locks open so that they could carry on the meeting for souls. God awoke the jailer out of his sleep and he was saved that night and all his house was saved.

Home is a place where character is fashioned. If the Lord rules the home, all will be right. Home is a place where father and mother are found; where children are born and reared. It is a community of persons, self-governed, or a kingdom within itself. It is an organization formed by God Himself. The home is a sacred place which should be godly.

Our preachers, statesmen, governors, and president come from the home. When Moses was found, Pharoah's daughter said,"Take this child away and nurse it for me and I will give thee thy wages." This is God's word to every mother. "Take this child and raise it for God and He will pay us in glory, for we don't know what He will be for God. We should be more careful in rearing our children. Although many homes have not children, they should be Christian homes just the same so that God would make them blessings to those who enter in them.

Marriage

We do not prohibit our people from marrying persons who are not of our church, provided such persons have the new birth, and are seeking the power of godliness; but we are determined to discourage their marrying persons who do not come up to this description. Many of our members have married unawakened persons. This has produced bad effects; they have been either hindered for life, or have turned back to perdition.

To discourage such marriages, let every minister publicly enforce the apostle's caution, "Be ye not unequally yoked together with unbelievers" (2 Cor. 6: 14). Also, let all be exhorted to take no step in so weighty a matter without advising (consulting for advice, *Ed.*) with the more serious of their brethren.

In general a woman ought not to marry without the consent of her parents. Yet there may be exceptions. For if, a woman believes it to be her duty to marry; and if her parents absolutely refuse to let her marry any Christian; then, she may, nay, ought to marry without their consent. Yet even then a minister ought not to be married to her.

How Sacred Is the Marriage Tie

No remarriage while the first part of the first covenant is living.

"And the third day there was a marriage in Cana of Galilee; and the mother of Jesus was there: and both Jesus was called, and His disciples, to the marriage. And when they wanted wine, the mother of Jesus saith unto Him. They have no wine. Jesus saith unto her, Woman, what have I to do with thee? mine hour is not yet come.

"His mother saith unto the servants, Whatsoever He saith unto you do it.

"And there were set there six waterpots of stone, after the manner of the purifying of the Jews, containing two or three firkins apiece. Jesus saith unto them, Fill the waterpots with water. And they filled them up to the brim. And He saith unto them, Draw out now, and bear unto the governor of the feast. And they bare it.

"When the ruler of the feast had tasted the water that was made wine, and knew not whence it was: (but the servants which drew the water knew;) the governor of the feast called the bridegroom, and saith unto him, Every man at the beginning doth set forth good wine; and when men have well drunk, then that which is worse, but thou hast kept the good wine until now" (John 2:1-10). Jesus has the best wine, His Spirit.

"This beginning of miracles did Jesus in Cana of Galilee, and manifested forth His glory; and His disciples believed on Him.

"And after this He went down to Capernaum, He, and His mother, and His brethren, and His disciples; and they continued there not many days" (John 2:11, 12).

"And the Lord God said. It is not good that the man should be alone; I will make him a help meet for him.

"And out of the ground the Lord God formed every beast of the field, and every fowl of the air; and brought them unto Adam to see what he would call them: and whatsoever Adam called every living creature, that was the name thereof.

"And Adam gave names to all cattle, and to the fowl of the air, and to every beast of the field; but for Adam there was not found an help meet for him.

"And the Lord God caused a deep sleep to fall upon Adam, and he slept; and he took one of his ribs, and closed up the flesh instead thereof; and the rib, which the Lord God had taken from man, made He a woman, and brought her unto the man. And Adam said, This is now bone of my bones, and flesh of my flesh; she shall be called Woman, because she was taken out of Man.

"Therefore, shall a man leave his father and his mother, and shall cleave unto his wife: and they shall be one flesh" (Genesis 2:18-24).

"The Pharisees also came unto him, tempting him, and saying unto him. Is it lawful for a man to put away his wife for every cause?

"And He answered and said unto them, Have ye not read, that He which made them at the beginning made them male and female, and said, For this cause shall a man leave father and mother, and shall cleave to his wife: and they twain shall be one flesh?

"Wherefore they are no more twain, but one flesh. What therefore God hath joined together, let not man put asunder. They say unto him, Why did Moses then command to give a writing of divorcement, and to put her away?

"He saith unto them, Moses because of the hardness of your hearts suffered you to put away your wives; but from the beginning it was not so" (Matt. 19: 3-8).

"And Jesus answered and said unto them, For the hardness of your heart He wrote you this precept. But, from the beginning of the creation God made them male and female. For this cause shall man leave his father and mother, and cleave to his wife; and they twain shall be one flesh; so then they are no more twain, but one flesh. What therefore God hath joined together, let not man put asunder.

"And in the house his disciples asked him again of the same matter. And He saith unto them, Whosoever shall put away his wife, and marry another, commiteth adultery against her. And if a woman shall put away her husband, and be married to another, she committeth adultery" (Mark 10: 5-12).

"Wives, submit yourselves unto your own husbands, as unto the Lord. For the husband is the head of the wife, even as Christ is the head of the church: and He is the saviour of the body.

"Therefore as the church is subject unto Christ, so let the wives be to their own husbands in everything. Husbands, love your wives, even as Christ also loved the church, and gave Himself for it: that He might sanctify and cleanse it with the washing of water by the word, that He might present it to Himself a glorious church, not having spot, or wrinkle, or any such thing; but that it should be holy and without blemish.

"So ought men to love their wives as their own bodies. He that loveth his wife loveth himself, for no man ever yet hated his own flesh; but nourisheth and cherisheth it, even as the Lord the church: for we are members of His body, of His flesh, and of His bones.

"For this cause shall a man leave his father and mother, and shall be joined unto his wife, and they two shall be one flesh. This is a great mystery: but I speak concerning Christ and the church.

"Nevertheless let every one of you in particular so love his wife even as himself; and the wife see that she reverence her husband" (Eph. 5:22-33).

"Wives, submit yourselves unto your own husbands, as it is fit in the Lord; Husbands, love your wives, and be not bitter against them" (Col. 3: 18-19).

Unscriptural Marriages

I. To marry a second companion while a former lives is adultery–sin–and is forbidden (Mark 7:2,3; 10:11,12).

II. To marry a person who has a living companion is adultery–sin–and is forbidden (Matt. 5:23; Luke 16:18; 1 John 3:4).

  1. The above is the law of Christ, and sin is the transgression of the law (1 John 3:4).

  2. To transgress God's law man must have a knowledge of that law.

    (a). Where no law is, there is no transgression (Rom. 4:15).

    (b). Sin is not imputed where there is no law (Rom. 5:13).

    (c). When men have no knowledge of God's law, they have no sin (John 15:22-24; John 9:39-41).

    (d). Light brings condemnation, but where no light is there is no condemnation (John 3:19).

  3. From the foregoing Scripture we learn that sin is a willful transgression of God's law. To commit sin men must have a knowledge of God's law, and transgress it knowingly, either the written law or the law of their conscience (Rom. 2:14-16).

III. Men who have a knowledge of the teachings of Christ's law regarding marriage, and then with that knowledge marry a second living companion, or a divorced wife or husband while their former companion lives, willfully transgress the law and are guilty before God of sin–adultery–and must forsake their sin (1 John 1:9; 3:4). If we confess our sins He will pardon us. All such unscriptural marriages must be dissolved to get clear from the sinful state of adultery (Prov. 28:13; Isa. 1:16, 17; 1 John 3:4; Gal. 5:19-21; 1 Cor. 6:9, 10).*

---

* Almost no one today would agree with this severe stand on divorce. It is certainly not the policy or doctrinal position of Christian Life Books.

IV. If men entered the unscriptural marriages, even though ignorant of the written law, yet condemned by the law of their conscience, such are not clear before God (Rom. 2:12, 14-16).

V. People who have entered unscriptural marriages in total ignorance of the teachings of Christ, and whose conscience did not condemn them because of the general low plane of teaching on this subject throughout the world, such individuals committed no sin–until the light came and they fail to walk in the light (John 3:19). The Bible says, "He that covereth his sin shall not prosper; but whosoever confesseth and forsaketh them shall have mercy (Prov. 28:13; 1 John 1:9).

Separation

I. Concerning divorce
1. There were no divorces in the beginning (Matt. 19:3-8)
2. Moses allowed men to put away their wives for any cause. If she found no favor in her husband's eyes; if he saw any unbecoming thing in her he could give her a bill of divorcement, send her away, and she might become another man's wife (Deut. 24:1-4; Matt. 19:7, 8)
3. Moses suffered men to divorce their wives and marry again because of the hardness of their hearts (Matt. 19:7, 8)
4. Jesus did away with the divorce law, and restored matrimony back to the Edenic standard (Matt. 19:3-8)

5. Under the New Testament, no court on earth should dissolve the marriage relation (Mark 10:2-9; Matt. 19:5-6)
6. Under the New Testament, husband and wife are bound together for life. Death alone severs the marriage tie (Rom. 7:2-3; 1Cor. 7:39)
7. Under the New Testament, there is but one cause for which a man can put away his wife.
8. After a man has lawfully put away his wife, or a wife has lawfully put away her husband, they are positively forbidden to marry again until the former companion is dead (Mark 10:11, 12; Luke 16:18; Rom. 7:2, 3)

II. Concerning departing
1. Let the wife not depart from her husband (1 Cor. 7:10)

Adultery
(Hebrews 13:4)

I. Under the New Testament, adultery implies:
1. An act of adultery (John 8:4)
2. A hidden lust of the heart (Matt. 5:28)
3. A state (Matt. 19:9)

II. The act of adultery is:
1. Coition between a married person and the opposite sex who is not the lawful companion. Both parties may be married, or only one.
2. This act is also called fornication (1 Cor. 5:1-13; Matt. 19:9; Matt. 5:32)

III. Secret adultery is as follows:
1. Looking on a woman to lust after her (Matt. 5:28; 2 Peter 2:14)

2. The secret lust and thought of the heart (Gen. 6:5; Mark 7:21-23)

IV. The state of adultery is as follows:
1. After putting a companion away, if the husband or wife marries another, while the first one lives, they are guilty of adultery (Mark 10:11, 12; Luke 16:18; 1 Cor. 7:39; Rom. 7:2, 3)
2. Whosoever marries a man or woman who has been put away is guilty of adultery (Matt. 5:32; Luke 16:18)

V. No man in adultery can enter Christ's kingdom without confessing and forsaking his sin (Gal. 5:19-2; Isa. 55:7)

Duties of Parents

I. The duty of parents to their children
1. They should love them (Titus 2:4)
2. They should train them up for God (Prov. 22:6; Eph. 6:4)
3. They should instruct them in God's word (Deut. 4:9; Deut. 11:19; Isa. 38:19)
4. They should rule them (1Tim. 3:4,12)
5. They should correct them (Prov. 13:24; Prov. 19:18; Prov. 23:13; Prov. 12:7)

II. Good parents:
1. Pity their children (Psa. 103:13)
2. Provide for their children (2 Cor. 12:14; 1Tim. 5:8)
3. Pray for their children (1 Chr. 29:19; Job 1:5; John 4:46-49)

Duty of Children

I. Children are:
1. A blessing (Prov. 10:1; Prov. 15:20; Prov.17:6; Psalm 128:1-4)
2. A gift from God (Psalm 127:3; Gen. 33:5)

II. The duty of children
1. They should obey God (Deut. 30:2)
2. They should seek God early (Eccl. 12:1)
3. They should attend to parental teaching (Prov. 1:8, 9)
4. They should honor their parents (Heb. 12:9)
5. They should obey their parents (Prov. 6:20-23; Eph. 6:1-3)
6. They should take care of their parents (1 Tim. 5:4)

III. Good children
1. Observe the law of God (Prov. 28:7)
2. Shall be blessed (Prov. 3:1-6)
3. Show love to their parents (Gen. 46:29)

Miscellaneous

Slavery

We declare that we are as much as ever convinced of the great evil of slavery. We believe that the buying, selling, or holding of human beings, to be used as chattles, is contrary to the laws of God and nature, and inconsistent with the golden rule, and with that rule in our discipline which requires all who desire to continue among us to "do no harm," and to "avoid evil of every kind." We therefore affectionately admonish all our ministers and people to keep themselves pure from this great evil, and to seek its extirpation by all lawful and Christian means.*

Educational Institutions

Our preachers must take a course of studies as the bishop shall prescribe later on. The educational

---

*The section is borrowed from an early discipline of the Methodist Episcopal Church. It is interesting that Seymour would include this, since slavery had been illegal in the United States for more than fifty years. Perhaps, this illustrates the impact that the peculiar institution had on Seymour, whose parents were both slaves in Louisiana prior to the Civil War. *Ed.*

institutions under the patronage of the church shall be classified as follows:

1. Primary schools
2. Secondary schools
3. Colleges
4. Universities
5. Schools of theology
6. Apostolic Faith or Bible schools

In mission fields and other localities where inadequate provision has been made for elementary instruction, primary schools may be established. *

---

*To the knowledge of the editor, neither Seymour nor any members of his fellowship ever established any of the schools mentioned here. Seymour, himself, had very limited formal education and that was probably in a Freedman's school in Louisiana. The first sentence, however, does indicate that he had a vision for educational institutions. Perhaps the last type of school mentioned would be similar to Charles Parham's Apostolic Faith school in Houston, Texas where Seymour attended and learned about the baptism in the Holy Ghost.

Forms and Church Ceremonies

The Lord's Supper Night

On the Lord's Supper night or day, the minister may preach the Lord's Supper sermon and, after he has preached the sermon, he can read 1 Cor. 11:23-32, to his people and give the supper. We always have the supper on Sunday night, and the feet washing on Thursday night before the Lord's Supper.

The Ordinance of Feet Washing

Then shall the minister say on the night or day when they gather to wash feet, "Dear Beloved Brethren, we have gathered here in the name of our Lord Jesus Christ to partake in this holy and sacred ordinance of foot washing which our Lord instituted on the same night He instituted the Lord's Supper, so we count it a happy night or day to carry it out. For our Lord said, 'Ye call Me Master and Lord, and ye say well; for so I am. If I am then, your Lord and master have washed your feet; ye also ought to wash one another's feet. For I have given you an example, that ye should do as I have done to

123

you. Verily, verily, I say unto you, the servant is not greater than his Lord; neither he that is sent greater than He that sent him. If ye know these things, happy are ye if ye do them' (John 13:13-17)."

Then the minister shall say to his people, "This is the Master's saying, so we will obey it."

Then shall he say, "Christ so loved the church, that He gave Himself for it, that He might present unto Himself a glorious church without spots or wrinkle, or any such thing; but that it should be holy and without blemish. So, when we wash each other's feet we acknowledge that we are washed in the blood of Jesus, and have pure hearts, and love each other. Foot washing gives every member a chance to examine himself before taking the Lord's Supper, so he can wash all the stripes like the Philippian jailer (Acts 16:21). That is to say, if we wrong any we will be willing to humble ourselves."

The minister can read John 13 and comment on it as the Lord gives words to say, in harmony with the ordinance.

Reception of Members

Form For Receiving Persons into the Church as Probationers

Those who are received into the church as probationers shall be called forward by name, and the minister, addressing the congregation shall say, "Dearly beloved brethren, that none may be admitted hastily into the church, we receive all persons seeking fellowship with us on profession of faith unto a preparatory membership on trial; in which proof may be made, both to themselves and to the church of the sincerity and depth of their convictions and of the strength of their purpose to lead a new life in Christ.

"The persons here present desire to be so admitted. You will hear their answers to the questions put to them, and if you make no objections they will be received (Acts 6:4).

"It is needful, however, that you be reminded of your responsibility, as having previously entered this holy fellowship, and as now representing the church into which they seek admission. Remembering their inexperience and how much they must learn in order to become good soldiers of Jesus Christ, see to it that they find in you holy examples of life and loving help in the true serving of their Lord and ours. I beseech you so to order your own lives that these new disciples may take no detriment from you, but that it may ever be cause for thanksgiving to God that they were led into this fellowship."

Then, addressing the persons seeking admission on probation, the minister shall say, "Dearly beloved, you have, by the grace of God, made your decision to follow Christ and to serve Him. Your confidence in so doing is not to be based on any notion of fitness or worthiness in yourselves, but solely on the merits of our Lord Jesus Christ, and on His death and intercession for us. That the church may know your purpose, you will answer the questions I am now to ask you."

The bishop. Have you an earnest desire to be saved from all your sins? Do you desire to be holy and wholly sanctified to God? Do you desire to be filled with the Holy Spirit?

Answer. I do.

The bishop. Will you guard yourselves against all things contrary to the teaching of God's word, and endeavor to lead a holy life, following the commandments of God?

Answer. I will endeavor so to do by His grace.

The bishop. Are you purposed to give reverent attendance upon the appointed means of grace in the ministry of the word, and in the public and private worship of God?

Answer. I am so determined, with the help of God.

The bishop. No objection being offered the minister shall then announce that the candidates are admitted as probationers and shall assign them to the watch care of the church. Then shall the minister offer extemporary prayer for the people that are coming into the church, as the Holy Spirit moves on him to pray.

Form for Receiving Persons into the Church after Probation

On the day appointed all that are to be received into the church shall be called forward and the minister addressing the congregation shall say, "Dearly beloved brethren, the scriptures teach us that the church is the household of God, the body of which Christ is head; and that it is the design of the gospel to bring together in one all who are in Christ. The fellowship of the church is the communion that its members enjoy one with another. The ends of this fellowship are the maintenance of sound doctrine and of the ordinances of Christian worship, and the exercise of that power of godly admonition and discipline which Christ has committed to his church for the promotion of holiness. It is the duty of all men to unite in this fellowship, for it is only those that 'be planted in the house of the Lord' that 'shall flourish in the courts of our God.' Its more particular duties are, to promote peace and unity; to bear one another's burdens; to prevent each other's stumbling; to seek the intimacy of friendly society among themselves; to continue steadfast in the faith and worship of the gospel; and to pray and sympathize with each other. Among its privileges are, peculiar incitements to holiness from the hearing of God's word and the sharing in God's ordinances; the being placed under the watchful care of pastors; and the enjoyment of the blessings which are promised only to those who are of the household of faith. Into this holy fellowship the persons before you who have already received the sacrament of the Lord's Supper and of baptism and the ordinance of foot washing, and have been born of the Spirit and have been under the care of proper leaders for six months on trial, come seeking admission. We now purpose in the fear of God to question them as to their faith and purposes, that you may know that they are proper persons to be admitted into the church (Acts 20:28-32)."

Then addressing the applicants for admission the minister shall say, "Dearly beloved, you are come hither seeking the great privilege of union with the church our Saviour has purchased with His own blood. We rejoice in the grace of God vouchsafed unto you in that He has called you to be His followers, and that thus far you have run well. You have heard how blessed are the privileges, and how solemn are the duties of membership in Christ's church; and before you are fully admitted thereto, it is proper that you do here publicly renew your vows, confess your faith, and declare your purpose, by answering the following questions."

The bishop. Do you here, in the presence of God and of this congregation, renew the solemn promise contained in the baptismal covenant, ratifying and confirming the same, and acknowledging yourselves bound faithfully to observe and keep that covenant?

Answer. I do.

The bishop. Have you saving faith in the Lord Jesus Christ?

Answer. I know I have in his blood.

The bishop. Do you believe in the doctrines of the holy scriptures as set forth in the articles of religion of the Apostolic Faith Church?

Answer. I do.

The bishop. Will you cheerfully be governed by the rules of the Apostolic Faith Church? Hold sacred the ordinances of God, and endeavor, as much as in you lies, to promote the welfare of your brethren and the advancement of the Redeemer's kingdom?

Answer. I will by His grace.

The bishop. Will you contribute of your earthly substance, according to your ability, to the support of the gospel and the various benevolent enterprises of the church?

Answer. I will.

Then the minister addressing the church shall say, "Brethren, these persons have given satisfactory responses to our inquiries, have any of you reason to allege why they should not be received into full membership in the church?"

No objections being alleged the minister shall say to the candidates, "We welcome you to the communion of the church of God; and, in testimony of our Christian affection and the cordiality with which we receive you, I hereby extend to you the right hand of fellowship; and may God grant that you may be a faithful and useful member of the church militant until you are called to the fellowship of the church triumphant, which is without fault before the throne of God."

Then shall the minister offer extemporary prayer, for the members received into the church and have members to shake their hands.

Consecration and Ordination of our Elders and Bishops

Elder and bishop are of the same rank, only differ in their office work. (This service is not to be understood as an ordination to a higher order in the Christian ministry, beyond and above that of elders or presbyters, but as a solemn and fitting consecration for the special and most sacred duties of superintendency in the church). The elder need not be confined to this prayer according to form, but let him pray it in the Spirit. *

The Form for Consecrating Bishops

The Collect

Almighty God, who by Thy Son Jesus Christ didst give the holy apostles, elders, and evangelists many excellent gifts, and didst charge them to feed Thy flock; give grace, we beseech thee, to all the ministers and pastors of the church, that they may diligently preach Thy word and duly administer the godly discipline thereof; and grant to the people that they may obediently fol-

*This form is borrowed from the Methodists, but this paragraph is original with Seymour.

low the same, that all may receive the crown of everlasting glory, through Jesus Christ our Lord. Amen.

The Epistle

Then shall be read by one of the elders Acts 20:17-35, "From Miletus Paul sent to Ephesus, and called the elders of the Church. And when they were come to him, he said unto them, Ye know, from the first day that I came to Asia, after what manner I have been with you at all seasons, serving the Lord with all humility of mind, and with many tears, and temptations, which befell me by the lying in wait of the Jews; and how I kept back nothing that was profitable unto you, but have showed you, and have taught you publicly, and from house to house, testifying both to the Jews, and also to the Greeks, repentance toward God, and faith toward our Lord Jesus Christ. And now, behold, I go bound in the spirit unto Jerusalem, not knowing the things that shall befall me there; save that the Holy Ghost witnesseth in every city, saying that bonds and afflictions abide me. But none of these things move me, neither count I my life dear unto myself, so that I might finish my course with joy, and the ministry, which I have received of the Lord Jesus, to testify the gospel of the grace of God.

"And now, behold, I know that ye all, among whom I have gone preaching the kingdom of God, shall see my face no more. Wherefore I take you to record this day, that I am pure from the blood of all men. For I have not shunned to declare unto you all the counsel of God. Take heed therefore unto yourselves, and to all the flock, over the which Holy Ghost hath made you overseers, to feed the church of God, which He hath purchased with His own blood.

For I know this, that after my departing shall grievous wolves enter in among you, not sparing the flock.

Also of your own selves shall men arise, speaking perverse things, to draw away disciples after them. Therefore watch, and remember, that by the space of three years I ceased not to warn everyone night and day with tears. And now, brethren, I commend you to God, and to the word of His grace, which is able to build you up, and give you an inheritance among all them which are sanctified. I have coveted no man's silver, or gold, or apparel. Yea, ye yourselves know, that these hands have ministered unto my necessities, and to them that were with me. I have showed you all things, how that so laboring ye ought to support the weak, and to remember the words of the Lord Jesus, how He said, It is more blessed to give than to receive."

The Gospel

Then another shall read John 21:15-17, "Jesus saith to Simon Peter, Simon, son of Jonas, lovest thou Me more than these? He saith unto him, Yea, Lord; thou knowest that I live Thee. He saith unto him, Feed My lambs. He saith to him again the second time, Simon, son of Jonas, lovest thou Me? He saith unto him, Yea, Lord; thou knowest that I love Thee. He saith unto him, Feed My sheep. He saith unto him the third time, Simon, son of Jonas, lovest thou Me? Peter was grieved because He said unto him the third time, Lovest thou Me? And he said unto Him, Lord, thou knowest all things; Thou knowest that I love Thee. Jesus saith unto him, Feed My sheep."

Or this, Matthew 28:18-20, "Jesus came and spake unto them, saying, All power is given unto Me in heaven and in earth. Go ye therefore, and teach all nations, baptizing them in the name of the Father, and of the Son, and of the Holy Ghost: teaching them to observe all things whatsoever I have commanded you; and, lo, I am with you always, even unto the end of the world."

After the gospel and the sermon are ended, the elected person shall be presented by two elders unto the bishop, saying, "We present unto you this holy man to be consecrated a bishop."

Then the bishop shall move the congregation present to pray, saying thus to them, "Brethren, it is written in the Gospel of Saint Luke that our Saviour Christ continued the whole night in prayer before He did choose and send forth His twelve Apostles. It is written also in the Acts of the Apostles that the disciples who were at Antioch did fast and pray before they laid hands on Paul and Barnabas, and sent forth on their first mission to the Gentiles. Let us therefore, following the example of our Saviour Christ, and His apostles, first fall to prayer before we admit and send forth this person presented to us to the work whereunto we trust the Holy Ghost hath called him."

As the Holy Spirit shall move to pray then shall the following prayer be offered,* "Almighty God, Giver of all good things, who by Thy Holy Spirit hast appointed divers offices in Thy Church: mercifully behold this Thy servant now called to the work and ministry of a bishop, and replenish him so with the truth of Thy doctrine, and adorn him with innocency of life, that both by word and deed he may faithfully serve Thee in this office, to the glory of Thy name, and the edifying and well governing of Thy church, through the merits of our Saviour Jesus Christ, who liveth and reigneth with Thee and the Holy Ghost, world without end. Amen."

Then the bishop shall say to him that is to be consecrated, "Brother, forasmuch as the holy scriptures

---

*The prayer is from the Methodist Discipline, the introduction referencing the Holy Spirit is from Seymour.

command that we shall not be hasty in laying on hands and admitting any person to government in the church of Christ, which He hath purchased with no less price than the shedding of His own blood; before you are admitted to this administration, you will, in the fear of God, give answer to the questions which I now propound."

The bishop. Are you persuaded that you are truly called to this ministration, according to the will of our Lord Jesus Christ?

Answer. I am so persuaded.

The bishop. Are you persuaded that the holy scriptures contain sufficiently all doctrines required of necessity for eternal salvation, through faith in Jesus Christ? And, are you determined out of the same holy scriptures to instruct the people committed to your charge, and to teach or maintain nothing as required of necessity to eternal salvation but that which you shall be persuaded may be concluded and proved by the same?

Answer. I am so persuaded and determined, by God's grace.

The bishop. Will you then faithfully exercise yourself in the same holy scriptures, and call upon God by prayer for the true understanding of the same, so that you may be able by them to teach and exhort with wholesome doctrine, and to withstand and convince the gainsayers? (Titus 1:9).

Answer. I will do so, by the help of God.

The bishop. Are you ready with faithful diligence to banish and drive away all erroneous and strange doctrines contrary to God's word, and both privately and openly to call upon and encourage others to the same?

Answer. I am ready, the Lord being my helper.

The bishop. Will you deny all ungodliness and worldly lust, and live soberly, righteously, and godly in this present world, that you may show yourself in all things an example of good works unto others, that the adversary may be ashamed, having nothing to say against you?

Answer. I will do so, the Lord being my helper.

The bishop. Will you maintain and set forward, as much as shall lie in you, quietness, love, and peace among all men; and such as shall be unjust, disobedient, and criminal, correct and punish according to such authority as you have by God's word, and as shall be committed unto you?

Answer. I will do so, by the help of God.

The bishop. Will you be faithful in ordaining, or laying hands upon and sending others, and in all the other duties of your office?

Answer. I will so be, by the help of God.

The bishop. Will you show yourself gentle, and be merciful, for Christ's sake, to poor and needy people, and to all strangers destitute of help?

Answer. I will so show myself, by God's help.

Then the bishop shall say, "Almighty God, our heavenly Father, who hath given you a good will to do all these things, grant also unto you strength and power to perform the same, that He accomplishing in you the good work which He has begun, you may be found blameless at the last day, through Jesus Christ our Lord. Amen."

That ended, the bishop shall say, "Lord, hear our prayer."

Answer. And let our cry come unto Thee.

The bishop shall then say, "Let us pray. Almighty and Most Merciful Father, who of Thine infinite goodness has given Thine only and dearly beloved Son Jesus Christ to be our Redeemer, and the author or everlasting life; who, after He had made perfect our redemption by His death, and was ascended into heaven, pouring down His gifts abundantly upon men, making some apostles, some prophets, some evangelists, some pastors and teachers, to the edifying and making perfect of His church. Grant, we beseech Thee, to this Thy servant, such grace that he may evermore be ready to spread abroad Thy gospel, the glad tidings of reconciliation with Thee, and use the authority given him, not to destruction but to salvation; not to hurt, but to help; so that as a wise and faithful servant, giving to the family their portion in due season, he may at last be received into everlasting joy, through Jesus Christ our Lord, who, with Thee and the Holy Ghost, liveth and reigneth, one God, world without end. Amen."

Then the bishop and elders present shall lay their hands upon the head of the elected person, kneeling before them, the bishop saying, "The Lord pour upon thee the Holy Ghost for the office and work of a bishop or elder in the church of God now committed unto thee by the authority of the church through the imposition of our hands, in the name of the Father, and of the Son, and of the Holy Ghost. Amen.

"And remember that thou stir up the grace of God which is in thee; for God hath not given us the spirit of fear, but of power, and love, and of a sound mind."

Then shall the bishop deliver to him the Bible, saying, "Give heed unto reading, exhortation, and doctrine. Think upon the things contained in this book. Be diligent in them, that the increase coming thereby may be manifest unto all men. Take heed unto thyself, and to thy doctrine; for by so doing thou shalt both save thyself and them that hear thee. Be to the flock of Christ a shepherd, not a wolf; feed them, devour them not. Hold up the weak, heal the sick, bind up the broken, bring again the outcast, seek the lost; be so merciful that you may not be too remiss; so minister discipline that you forget not mercy; that when the Chief Shepherd shall appear, you may receive the never-fading crown of glory, through Jesus Christ our Lord. Amen."

Then the bishop shall administer the Lord's Supper to the newly consecrated bishop and other persons present.

Then shall be offered the following prayers:

Most Merciful Father, we beseech Thee to send down upon this Thy servant the heavenly blessing, and to so endow him with Thy Holy Spirit that he, preaching Thy word, and exercising authority in Thy Church, may not only be earnest to reprove, beseech, and rebuke with all patience and doctrine, but also may be, to such as believe, a wholesome example in word, in conversation, in love, in faith, and in purity; that faithfully fulfilling his course, at the last day he may receive the crown of righteousness laid up by the Lord, the righteous Judge, who liveth and reigneth, one God with the Father and the Holy Ghost, world without end. Amen.

Prevent us, O Lord, in all our doings with Thy most gracious favor, and further us with Thy continual help, that in all our works, begun, continued, and ended in

Thee, we may glorify Thy holy name; and finally, by Thy mercy, obtain everlasting life , through Jesus Christ our Lord. Amen.

The peace of God, which passeth all understanding, keep your hearts and minds in the knowledge and love of God, and of His Son Jesus Christ our Lord: and the blessing of God Almighty, the Father, the Son, and the Holy Ghost, be among you, and remain with you always. Amen.

The Form for Ordaining Elders

When the day appointed by the bishop is come, there shall be a sermon or exhortation, declaring the duty and office of such as come to be admitted elders; how necessary that order is in the church of Christ, and also how the people ought to esteem the elders in their office.

After which, one of the elders shall present unto the bishop all them that are to be ordained, and say, "I present unto you these persons to be ordained as elders."

Then their names being read aloud, the bishop shall say to the people, "Brethren, these are they whom we purpose, God willing, this day to ordain elders. For after due examination, we find not to the contrary, but that they are lawfully called to this function and ministry, and that they are persons meet for the same. But, if there be any of you who knoweth any crime or impediment in any of them, for the which he ought not to be received into this holy ministry let him come forth in the name of God, and show what the crime or impediment is." (If any crime or impediment be objected, the bishop shall surcease from ordaining that person until such time as the party accused shall be found clear of the same).

Then shall be said the collect, epistle, and gospel. Now prayer can be offered as the Spirit give utterance in the Holy Spirit.

The Collect

Almighty God, giver of all good things, who by Thy Holy Spirit hast appointed divers orders of ministers in the church; mercifully behold these Thy servants now called to the office of elders, and replenish them so with the truth of Thy doctrine, and adorn them with innocency of life, that both by word and good example they may faithfully serve Thee in this office, to the glory of Thy name, and the edification of the church, through the merits of our Saviour Jesus Christ, who liveth and reigneth with Thee and the Holy Ghost, world without end. Amen.

The Epistle

Ephesians 4:7-13, "Unto every one of us is given grace according to the measure of the gift of Christ. Wherefore He saith, When He ascended up on high, He led captivity captive, and gave gifts unto men. Now that He ascended, what is it but that He also descended first into the lower parts of the earth? He that descended is the same also that ascended up far above all heavens, that He might fill all things. And He gave some, apostles; and some prophets; and some, evangelists; and some, pastors and teachers; for the perfecting of the saints, for the work of the ministry, for the edifying of the body of Christ; till we all come in the unity of the faith, and of the knowledge of the Son of God, unto a perfect man, unto the measure of the stature of the fullness of Christ."

The Gospel

After this shall be read for the gospel part of the tenth chapter of John 10:1-16, "Verily, verily, I say unto you. He that entereth not by the door into the sheep fold, but climbeth up some other way, the same is a thief and a robber. But he that entereth in by the door is the shepherd of the sheep. To him the porter openeth; and the sheep hear his voice; and he calleth his own sheep by name, and leadeth them out. And when he putteth forth his own sheep, he goeth before them, and the sheep follow him; for they know his voice. And a stranger will they not follow, but will flee from him; for they know not the voice of strangers. This parable spake Jesus unto them; but they understood not what things they were which He spake unto them.

"Then said Jesus unto them again. Verily, verily, I say unto you, I am the door of the sheep. All that ever came before Me are thieves and robbers; but the sheep did not hear them. I am the door; by Me if any man enter in, he shall be saved, and shall go in and out, and find pasture. The thief cometh not but for to steal, and to kill, and to destroy: I am come that they might have life, and that they might have it more abundantly. I am the good shepherd: the good shepherd giveth His life for the sheep. But he that is a hireling, and not the shepherd, whose own the sheep are not, seeth the wolf coming, and leaveth the sheep, and fleeth; and the wolf catcheth them, and scattereth the sheep. The hireling fleeth, because he is a hireling, and careth not for the sheep. I am the good shepherd, and know My sheep, and am known of mine. As the Father knoweth Me, even so know I the Father; and I lay down My life for the sheep. And other sheep I have, which are not of this fold: them also I must bring, and they shall hear My voice; and there shall be one fold and one shepherd."

And that done, the bishop shall say unto the persons to be ordained elders, "You have heard, brethren, in your private examination, and in the holy lessons taken out of the gospel and the writings of the apostles, of what dignity and of how great importance this office is whereunto ye are called. And now again we exhort you, in the name of our Lord Jesus Christ, that ye have in remembrance into how high a dignity and to how weighty an office ye are called; that is to say, to be messengers, watchmen, and stewards of the Lord; to teach and to admonish, to feed and provide for, the Lord's family; to gather the outcasts, to seek the lost, and to be ever ready to spread abroad the gospel, the glad tidings of reconciliation with God.

"Have always therefore printed in your remembrance how great a treasure is committed to your charge. For they are the sheep of Christ, which He bought with His body. And if it shall happen, the same church, or any member thereof, do take any hurt or hindrance by reason of your negligence, ye know the greatness of the fault, and also the fearful punishment that will ensue. Wherefore consider with yourselves the end of the ministry toward the children of God, toward the spouse and body of Christ; and see that you never cease your labor, your care and diligence, until you have done all that lieth in you, according to your bounden duty, to bring all such as are or, shall be committed to your charge unto that agreement in the faith and knowledge of God, and to that ripeness and perfectness of age in Christ, that there be no place left among you either for error in religion or for viciousness in life.

"Forasmuch then as your office is both of so great excellency and of so great difficulty, ye see with how great care and study ye ought to apply yourselves, as well that ye may show yourselves dutiful and thankful unto that Lord who hath placed you in so high a dignity; as also to beware that neither you yourselves offend, nor be occasion that others offend. Howbeit ye cannot have a mind and will thereto of yourselves, for that will and ability are given of God alone; therefore ye ought, and have need, to pray earnestly for his Holy Spirit. And seeing that ye cannot by any other means compass the doing of so weighty a work, pertaining to the salvation of man, but with doctrine and exhortation taken out of the holy scriptures, and with a life agreeable to the same; consider how studious ye ought to be in reading and learning the scriptures, and in framing the manners, both of yourselves and of them that specially pertain unto you, according to the rule of the same scriptures; and for this selfsame cause, how ye ought to forsake and set aside, as much as you may, all worldly cares and studies.

"We have good hope that you have all weighed and pondered these things with yourselves long before this time; and that you have clearly determined, by God's grace, to give yourselves wholly to this office, whereunto it has pleased God to call you: so that, as much as lieth in you, you will apply yourselves wholly to this one thing, and draw all your cares and studies this way, and that you will continually pray to God the Father, by the meditation of our only Saviour Jesus Christ, for the heavenly assistance of the Holy Ghost; that by daily reading and weighing of the scriptures ye may wax riper and stronger in your ministry; and that ye may so endeavor to sanctify the lives of you and yours, and to fashion them after the rule and doctrine of Christ, that ye may be wholesome and godly examples and patterns for the people to follow.

And now, that this present congregation of Christ here assembled may also understand your minds and wills in these things, and that this your promise may the more move you to do your duties, ye shall answer plainly to these things which we, in the name of God and His church, shall demand of you touching the same."

The bishop. Do you think in your heart that you are truly called, according to the will of our Lord Jesus Christ, to the order of elders?

Answer. I think so.

The bishop. Are you persuaded that the holy scriptures contain sufficiently all doctrine required of necessity for eternal salvation through faith in Jesus Christ? And, are you determined out of the said scriptures to instruct the people committed to your charge, and to teach nothing as required of necessity to eternal salvation but that which you shall be persuaded may be concluded and proved by the scriptures?

Answer. I am so persuaded, and have so determined, by God's grace.

The bishop. Will you then give your faithful diligence always so to minister the doctrine, and sacraments and discipline of Christ, as the Lord hath commanded?

Answer. I will so do, by the help of the Lord.

The bishop. Will you be ready with all faithful diligence to banish and drive away all erroneous and strange doctrines contrary to God's word, and to use both public and private monitions and exhortations, as well to the sick as to the whole within your charge, as need shall require and occasion shall be given?

Answer. I will, the Lord being my helper.

The bishop. Will you be diligent in prayers, and in reading of the holy scriptures, and in such studies as help to the knowledge of the same, laying aside the study of the world and the flesh?

Answer. I will endeavor so to do, the Lord being my helper.

The bishop. Will you be diligent to frame and fashion yourselves, and your families, according to the doctrine of Christ; and to make both yourselves and them, as much as in you lieth, wholesome examples and patterns to the flock of Christ?

Answer. I will apply myself thereto, the Lord being my helper.

The bishop. Will you maintain and set forward, as much as lieth in you, quietness, peace, and love, among all Christian people, and especially among them that are or shall be committed to your charge?

Answer. I will so do, the Lord being my helper.

The bishop. Will you reverently obey your chief ministers, unto whom is committed the charge and government over you, following with a glad mind and will their godly admonitions, submitting yourselves to their godly judgments?

Answer. I will so do, the Lord being my helper.

Then shall the bishop, standing up, say, "Almighty God, who hath given you this will to do all these things, grant also unto you strength and power to perform the same that He may accomplish His work which He hath begun in you, through Jesus Christ our Lord. Amen."

After this the congregation shall be desired secretly, in their prayers to make their humble supplications to God for all these things; for which the prayers there shall be silence kept for a space.

After this has been said by the bishop, the persons to be ordained elders, all kneeling, the bishop beginning, and the elders and others that are present answering by verse, as followeth:

> Come, Holy Ghost, our souls inspire,
> And lighten with celestial fire.
> Thou the anointing Spirit art,
> Who dost Thy sevenfold gifts impart.
> Thy blessed unction from above
> Is comfort, life, and fire of love.
> Enable with perpetual light
> The dullness of our blinded sight;
> Anoint and cheer our soiled face
> With the abundance of thy grace;
> Keep far our foes, give peace at home;
> Where thou art Guide, no ill can come.
> Teach us to know the Father, Son,
> And Thee of both to be but *one*;
> That through the ages all along
> This may be our endless song:
> Praise to Thy eternal merit,
> Father, Son, and Holy Spirit.

That done, the bishop shall pray in this wise, and say, "Let us pray. Pray in the Holy Spirit.* Almighty God

---

* Seymour added the sentence about praying in the Holy Spirit. *Ed.*

and heavenly Father who of Thine infinite love and goodness toward us hast given to us Thine only and most dearly beloved Son Jesus Christ to be our redeemer, and the author of everlasting life; who, after He had made heaven, sent abroad into the world His apostles, prophets, evangelists, teachers, and pastors, by whose labor and ministry He gathered together a great flock in all parts of the world, to set forth the eternal praise of Thy holy name: for that then has vouchsafed to call these Thy servants here present to the same office and ministry appointed for the salvation of mankind, we render unto Thee most hearty thanks; we praise and worship thee; and we humbly beseech Thee by the same, Thy blessed Son, to grant unto all who either here or elsewhere call upon Thy name, that we may continue to show ourselves thankful unto thee for these, and all other thy benefits, and that we may daily increase and go forward in the knowledge and faith of Thee and Thy Son, by the Holy Spirit. So that as well by these Thy ministers, as by them over whom they shall be appointed Thy ministers, Thy holy name may be forever glorified, and Thy blessed kingdom enlarged, through the same, Thy Son, Jesus Christ our Lord, Who liveth and reigneth with Thee in the unity of the same Holy Spirit, world without end. Amen."

When this prayer is done, the bishop and the elders present shall lay their hands severally upon the head of every one that receiveth the order of elders; the receivers humbly kneeling, and the bishop saying, "The Lord pour upon thee the Holy Ghost for the office and work of an elder in the church of God, now committed unto thee by the authority of the church, through the imposition of our hands. And be thou a faithful dispenser of the word of God, and of His holy sacraments; in the name of the Father, and of the Son, and of the Holy Ghost. Amen."

Then the bishop shall deliver to every one of them, kneeling, the Bible into his hands, saying, "Take thou authority as an elder in the church to preach the word of God, and to administer the holy sacraments in the congregation."

These prayers are good let God lead. It must be from the heart and through the Holy Spirit. *

Then the bishop shall offer the following prayer, "Most merciful Father, we beseech Thee to send upon these Thy servants Thy heavenly blessings, that they may be clothed with righteousness, and that Thy word spoken by their mouths may have such success that it may never be spoken in vain. Grant also that we may have grace to hear and receive what they shall deliver out of Thy most holy word, or agreeably to the same, as the means of our salvation; and that in all our words and deeds we may seek Thy glory, and the increase of Thy kingdom, through Jesus Christ our Lord. Amen.

"Prevent us, O Lord, in all our doings, with Thy most gracious favor, and further us by Thy continual help; that in all our works, begun, continued, and ended it. Thee, we may glorify Thy holy name, and finally, by Thy mercy, obtain everlasting life through Jesus Christ our Lord. Amen.

"The peace of God, which passeth all understanding, keep your hearts and minds in the knowledge and love of God, and of His Son Jesus Christ our Lord; and the blessing of God Almighty, the Father, the Son, and the Holy Ghost, be among you, and remain with you always. Amen."

---

* This sentence was added by Seymour. *Ed.*

(If on the same day the order of deacons be given to some and that of elders to others, the deacons shall be first presented, and then the elders. The collect shall both be used; first that for deacons, then that for elders. The epistle shall be Ephesians 4:7-13, as before in this office. Immediately after which, they who are to be ordained deacons shall be examined and ordained as is below prescribed. Then one of them having read the gospel, which shall be John 10:1-16, as before in this office, they who are to be ordained elders shall likewise be examined and ordained, as in this office before appointed).

The Form for Ordaining Deacons

When the day appointed by the bishop is come, there shall be a sermon or exhortation, declaring the duty and office of such as come to be admitted to the order of deacons.

After which one of the elders shall present unto the bishop the persons to be ordained deacons, and their names being read aloud the bishop shall say unto the people, "Brethren, if there be any of you who knoweth any crime of impediment in any of these persons presented to be ordained deacons, for the which he ought not to be admitted to that office, let him come forth in the name of God, and show what the crime or impediment is."

The elder can use the prayer or let the Lord give him one as he may be led. If any crime of impediment be objected, the bishop shall surcease from ordaining that persons until such time as the party accused shall be found clear of the same.

Then shall be read the following collect and epistle:

The Collect

Almighty God, who by Thy divine providence hast appointed divers orders of ministers in Thy church, and didst inspire Thy apostles to chose into the order of deacons Thy first martyr, Saint Stephen, with others. Mercifully behold these Thy servants, now called to the like office and administration; replenish them so with the truth of Thy doctrine, and adorn them with innocency of life, that both by word and good example they may faithfully serve Thee in this office to the glory of Thy name, and the edification of Thy church, through the merits of our Saviour Jesus Christ, who liveth and reigneth with Thee and the Holy Ghost, now and forever. Amen.

The Epistle

1 Timothy 3:8-13, "Likewise must the deacons be grave, not double-tongued, not given to much wine, not greedy of filthy lucre; holding the mystery of the faith in a pure conscience. And let these also first be proved; then let them use the office of a deacon, being found blameless. Even so must their wives be grave, not slanderers, sober, faithful in all things. Let the deacons be the husbands of one wife, ruling their children and their own houses well. For they that have used the office of a deacon well purchase to themselves a good degree, and great boldness in the faith which is in Christ Jesus."

Then shall the bishop, in the presence of the people, examine every one of those who are to be ordained, after this manner following:

The bishop. Do you trust that you are inwardly moved by the Holy Ghost to take upon you the office of the ministry in the church of Christ, to serve God for the promoting of His glory and the edifying of His people?

Answer. I trust so.

The bishop. Do you unfeignedly believe all the canonical scriptures of the Old and New Testaments?

Answer. I do believe them.

The bishop. Will you diligently read or expound the same unto the people whom you shall be appointed to serve?

Answer. I will.

The bishop. It appertaineth to the office of a deacon to assist the elder in divine service, and especially when he ministereth the holy communion, to help him in the distribution thereof; to read and expound the holy scriptures; to instruct the youth; and to baptize. And furthermore, it is his office to search for the sick, poor, and impotent, that they may be visited and relieved. Will you do this gladly and willingly?

Answer. I do so, by the help of God.

The bishop. Will you apply all your diligence to frame and fashion your own lives and the lives of your families according to the doctrine of Christ; and to make both yourselves and them, as much as in you lieth, wholesome examples of the flock of Christ?

Answer. I will do so, the Lord being my helper.

The bishop. Will you reverently obey them to whom the charge and government over you is committed, following with a glad mind and will their godly admonitions?

Answer. I will endeavor so to do, the Lord being my helper.

Then the bishop, laying his hands severally upon the head of every one of them, shall say, "Take thou authority to execute the office of a deacon in the church of God; in the name of the Father, and of the Son, and of the Holy Ghost. Amen."

Then shall the bishop deliver to every one of them the Holy Bible, saying "Take thou authority to read the holy scriptures in the church of God, and to preach the same."

Then one appointed by the bishop shall read the gospel.

The Gospel

Luke 12:35-38, "Let your loins be girdled about, and your lights burning; and ye yourselves like unto men that wait for their lord, when he will return from the wedding; that, when he cometh and knocketh, they may open unto him immediately. Blessed are those servants, whom the lord when he cometh shall find watching: verily I say unto you, that he shall gird himself, and make them to sit down to meat, and will come forth and serve them. And if he shall come in the second watch, or come in the third watch, and find them so, blessed are those servants."

The elder may use this prayer if he desire, or pray as the Holy Spirit move him.* Immediately before the benediction shall be said these collects following:

---

* Added by Seymour. *Ed.*

Almighty God, giver of all good things, who of Thy great goodness has vouchsafed to accept and take these Thy servants into the office of deacons in the church; make them, we beseech thee, O Lord, to be modest, humble, and constant in their ministration, and to have a ready will to observe all spiritual discipline; that they, have always the testimony of a good conscience, and continuing ever stable and strong in Thy Son Christ, may so well behave themselves in this inferior office that they may be found worthy to be called into the higher ministries in Thy church, through the same, thy Son our Saviour Jesus Christ; to whom be glory and honor, world without end. Amen.

Prevent us, O Lord, in all our doings, with Thy most gracious favor, and further us with Thy continual help; that in all our works, begun, continued, and ended in Thee, we may glorify Thy holy name, and finally, by Thy mercy, obtain everlasting life, through Jesus Christ our Lord. Amen.

The peace of God, which passeth all understanding, keep your hearts and minds in the knowledge and love of God, and of His Son Jesus Christ our Lord. And, the blessing of God Almighty, the Father, the Son, and the Holy Ghost, be among you, and remain with you always. Amen.

Solemnization of Matrimony

First, the bans of all that are to be married together, must be published in the congregation three several Sundays in the time of divine service, unless they be otherwise qualified according to law, the minister saying, after the accustomed manner, "I publish these bans of marriage between (name of groom) of (place of residence) and (name of bride) of (place of residence). If any of you know just cause or impediment why these two persons should not be joined in holy matrimony, you are to declare it. This is the first, (second, or third) time of asking."

At the day and time appointed for the solemnization, the persons to be married standing together, the man on the right side and the woman on the left, the minister shall say, "Dearly beloved, we are gathered together here in the sight of God, and in the presence of these witnesses, to join together this man and this woman in holy matrimony; which is an honorable estate, instituted by God in the time of man's innocency, signifying unto us the mystical union which is between Christ and His church: which holy estate Christ adorned and beautified with His presence, and first miracle that He wrought at Cana of Galilee, and is commended of St. Paul to be honorable among all men, and therefore not by any to be entered upon or taken in hand unadvisedly, but reverently, discreetly, advisedly, and in the fear of God.

"Into which holy estate these persons come now to be joined. Therefore if any can show any just cause why they may not lawfully be joined together, let him now speak, or else hereafter forever hold his peace."

And also speaking to the persons that are to be married, he shall say, "I require and charge you both, as you will answer at the dreadful day of judgment, when the secrets of all hearts shall be disclosed that if either of you know any impediment why you may not be lawfully joined together in matrimony, you do now confess it; for be ye well assured that so many as are coupled together otherwise that God's word shall allow, are not joined together by God, neither is their matrimony lawful in the sight of God. For God's word forbids marrying to another while the first party of the first covenant are living (Malachi 2:14-16; Mark 10:11-12; Luke 16:18; Rom. 7:1-3)."*

If no impediment shall be alleged, then shall the minister say unto the man, "(Name of groom), wilt thou have this woman to be thy wedded wife, to live together after God's ordinance, in the holy state of matrimony? Wilt thou love her, comfort her, honor and keep her, in sickness and in health, and forsaking all others, keep thee only unto her, as long as ye both shall live?"

The man shall answer, "I will!"

Then shall the minister say unto the woman, "(Name of bride), wilt thou have this man to be thy wedded husband, to live together after God's ordinance in the holy state of matrimony? Wilt thou obey him, serve him, love him, and honor him, and reverence him and keep him, in sickness and in health; and forsake all others, keep thee only unto him so long as ye both shall live?"

The woman shall answer, "I will!"

The man with his right hand, taking the woman by her right hand, shall say after the minister, "I, (Name of the groom) take thee (Name of the bride), to be my wedded wife, to have and to hold, from this day forward, for better, or for worse, for richer, for poorer, in sickness and in health, to love and to cherish till death do us part, according to God's holy ordinance; and thereto I plight thee my faith."**

---

*Seymour added the last line and the scriptures. As other parts of the *Discipline* demonstrate, he was totally opposed to remarriage after divorce.

**The first 18 words of this paragraph were not part of the original. *Ed.*

Then they shall loose their hands, and the woman with her right hand, taking the man by his right hand, shall likewise say after the minister, "I, (Name of the bride) take thee (Name of the groom), to be my wedded husband, to have and to hold, from this day forward, for better, for worse, for richer, for poorer, in sickness and in health, to love, cherish and to obey, till death do us part, according to God's holy ordinance; and thereto I plight thee my faith."

Then shall the minister say, "Let us pray. O, Eternal God, Creator, Preserver of all mankind, giver of all spiritual grace, the author of everlasting life; send Thy blessing upon these Thy servants, this man and this woman, whom we bless in Thy name; that as Isaac and Rebecca lived faithfully together, so these persons may surely perform and keep the vow and covenant betwixt them made, and may ever remain in perfect love and peace together, and live according to thy laws, through Jesus Christ our Lord, Amen."

If the parties desire it, the man shall here hand a ring to the minister, who shall return it to him and direct him to place it on the third finger of the woman's left hand. And the man shall say to the woman, repeating after the minister, "With this ring I thee wed, and with my worldly goods I thee endow, in the name of the Father, and of the Son, and of the Holy Ghost. Amen."

Then shall the minister join their right hands together and say, "Those whom God hath joined together, let no man put asunder.

"Forasmuch as (Name of groom) and (Name of bride) have consented to live together in holy wedlock and have witnessed the same before God and this company, and thereto have pledged their faith to each other, and have declared the same by joining hands: I pronounce that they are man and wife together, in the name of the Father, and of the Son, and of the Holy Ghost. Amen."

And the minister shall add this blessing, "God the Father, God the Son, and God the Holy Ghost, bless, preserve and keep you; the Lord mercifully with His favor look upon you and so fill you with all spiritual benediction and grace, that you may so live together in this life, that in the world to come ye may have life everlasting. Amen."

Then shall the minister say, "Our Father, who art in heaven, hallowed be Thy name. Thy kingdom come. Thy will be done on earth, as it is in heaven. Give us this day our daily bread. And forgive us our trespasses, as we forgive those who trespass against us. And lead us not into temptation; but deliver us from evil: for thine is the kingdom, the power, and the glory forever. Amen."

Then shall the minister say, "O God of Abraham, God of Isaac, God of Jacob, bless this man and woman, and sow the seeds of eternal life in their hearts, that whatsoever in Thy holy word they shall profitably learn, they may indeed fulfill the same. Look, O Lord, mercifully upon them from heaven and bless them. And as thou didst send Thy blessings upon Abraham and Sarah, to their great comfort, so vouchsafe to send Thy blessings upon this man and this woman, that they obeying Thy will, and always being in safety under Thy protection, may abide in Thy love unto their lives' end, through Jesus Christ our Lord. Amen.

"O God, who by Thy mighty power hast made all things of nothing, who also (after other things set in order), didst appoint that out of man (created after thine own image and similitude), woman should take her beginning; and knitting them together, didst teach that it should never be lawful to put asunder those whom Thou, by matrimony, hast made one; O God who has consecrated the state of matrimony to such an excellent mystery, that in it is signified and represented the spiritual marriage and union betwixt Christ and His church-look mercifully upon this man and this woman; that both this man may love his wife according to Thy word, (as Christ did love His spouse, the church, who gave Himself for it, loving and cherishing it even as His own flesh), and also that this woman may be loving and obedient to her husband; and in all quietness, sobriety and peace, be a follower of holy and godly matrons. O Lord, bless them both, and grant them to inherit Thy everlasting kingdom, through Jesus Christ our Lord. Amen."

Then shall the minister say, "Almighty God, who at the beginning didst create our first parents, Adam and Eve, and didst sanctify and join them together in marriage, pour upon you the riches of His grace, sanctify and bless you that ye may please Him both in body and soul, and live together in holy love unto your lives; end. Amen."

Burial of the Dead

We will on no account whatever make a charge for burying the dead.

Form for the Burial of the Dead

Any of these scriptures may be taken for the occasion.

"I am the resurrection, and the life; he that believeth in Me, though he were dead, yet shall he live; and whosoever liveth and believeth in Me shall he live: and whosoever liveth and believeth in Me shall never die" (John 11:25,26).

"I know that my redeemer liveth, and that He shall stand at the later day upon the earth: and though after my skin worms destroy this body, yet in my flesh shall I see God: whom I shall see for myself, and mine eyes shall behold, and not another" (Job 19:25-27).

"We brought nothing into this world, and it is certain we can carry nothing out. The Lord gave, and the Lord hath taken away; blessed be the name of the Lord" (1Tim. 6:7; Job 1:21).

In the house or church may be read one or both of the following Psalms, or some other suitable portion of the holy scriptures (we may read this at the unsaved but not at the saved),* "I said, I will take heed to my ways, that I sin not with my tongue: I will keep my mouth with a bridle, while the wicked is before me. I was dumb with silence. I held my peace, even from good; and my sorrow was stirred. My heart was hot within me; while I was musing the fire burned: then spake I with my tongue, Lord, make me to know mine end, and the measure of my days, what it is; that I may know how frail I am. Behold, Thou hast made my days as a handbreadth; and mine age is as nothing before thee; verily every man at his best state is altogether vanity. Surely every man walketh in a vain show: surely they are disquieted in vain: he heapeth up riches, and knoweth not who shall gather them. And now, Lord, what wait I for? My hope is in Thee. Deliver me from all my transgressions: make me not the reproach of the foolish. I was dumb, I opened not my mouth; because Thou didst it.

---

* This parenthetical was added by Seymour

Remove Thy stroke away from me; I am consumed by the blow of Thine hand. When thou with rebukes does correct man for iniquity, Thou makest his beauty to consume away like a moth; surely every man is vanity. Hear my prayer, O Lord, and give ear unto my cry; hold not Thy peace at my tears; for I am a stranger with Thee, and a sojourner, as all my fathers were. O spare me, that I may recover strength, before I go hence, and be no more" (Psalm 39).

Psalm 90, "Lord, Thou has been our dwelling place in all generations. Before the mountains were brought forth, or ever Thou hadst formed the earth and the world, even from everlasting to everlasting, Thou art God. Thou turnest man to destruction; and sayest, Return, ye children of men. For a thousand years in Thy sight are but as yesterday when it is past, and as a watch in the night. Thou carriest them away as with a flood; they are as a sleep; in the morning they are like grass which groweth up. In the morning it flourisheth, and groweth up; in the evening it is cut down, and withereth. For we are consumed by Thine anger, and by Thy wrath are we troubled. Thou hast set our iniquities before Thee, our secret sins in the light of Thy countenance. For all our days are passed away in Thy wrath; we spend our years as a tale that is told. The days of our years are threescore years and ten; and if by reason of strength they be four score years, yet is their strength labor and sorrow; for it is soon cut off, and we fly away. Who knoweth the power of Thine anger? even according to Thy fear, that we may apply our hearts unto wisdom. Return, O Lord, how long? and let it repent Thee concerning Thy servants. O satisfy us early with Thy mercy; that we may rejoice and be glad all our days. Make us glad according to the days wherein Thou hast afflicted us, and the years wherein we have seen evil. Let Thy work appear unto Thy servants, and Thy glory unto their children. And let the beauty of the Lord our God be upon us; and establish Thou the work of our hands upon us; yea, the work of our hands establish Thou it."

Then may follow the reading of the epistle, as follows:

1 Corinthians 15:41-58, "There is one glory of the sun, and another glory of the moon, and another glory of the stars; for one star differeth from another star in glory. So also is the resurrection of the dead. It is sown in corruption, it is raised in incorruption; it is sown in dishonor, it is raised in glory; it is sown in weakness, it is raised in power; it is sown a natural body, and is raised a spiritual body. And so it is written, The first man Adam was made a living soul; the last Adam was made a quickening spirit. Howbeit that was not first which is spiritual, but that which is natural; and afterward that which is spiritual. The first man is of the earth, earthy; the second man is the Lord from heaven. As is the earthy, such are they also that are earthy, and as is the heavenly, such are they also that are heavenly. And as we have borne the image of the earthy, we shall also bear the image of the heavenly. Now this I say, brethren, that flesh and blood cannot inherit the kingdom of God; neither doth corruption inherit incorruption. Behold, I show you a mystery; We shall not all sleep, but we shall all be changed, in a moment, in the twinkling of an eye, at the last trump: for the trumpet shall sound, and the dead shall be raised incorruptible, and we shall be changed. For this corruptible must put on incorruption, and this mortal must put on immortality, then shall be brought to pass the saying that is written, Death is swallowed up in victory. O death, where is thy sting? O grave, where is thy victory? The sting of death is sin; and the

strength of sin is the law. But thanks be to God, which giveth us the victory through our Lord Jesus Christ. Therefore, my beloved brethren, be ye steadfast, unmovable, always abounding in the work of the Lord, forasmuch as ye know that your labor is not in vain in the Lord."

At the grave, when the corpse is laid in the earth, the minister shall say, "Man that is born of a woman hath but a short time to live, and is full of misery. He cometh up, and is cut down like a flower: he fleeth as it were a shadow, and never continueth in one stay.

"In the midst of life we are in death; of whom may we seek for succor, but of Thee, O Lord, who for our sins are justly displeased?

"Yet, O Lord God most holy. O Lord most mighty, O holy and most merciful Saviour, deliver us not into the bitter pains of eternal death.

"Thou knowest, Lord, the secrets of our hearts; shut not Thy merciful ears to our prayers, but spare us, Lord most holy; O God most mighty, O holy and merciful Saviour, Thou most worthy judge eternal, suffer us not at our last hour for any pains of death to fall from Thee."

Then, while the earth shall be cast upon the body by some standing by, the minister shall say, "Forasmuch as it hath pleased Almighty God, in His wise providence, to take out of the world the soul of the departed, we therefore commit his body to the ground, earth to earth, ashes to ashes; dust to dust; looking for the general resurrection in the last day, and the life of the world to come, through our Lord Jesus Christ; at whose second coming in glorious majesty to judge the world, the earth and the sea shall give up their dead; and the corruptible bodies of those who sleep in Him shall be changed and made like unto His own glorious body; according to the mighty working whereby He is able to subdue all things unto Himself."

Then shall be said, "I heard a voice from heaven saying unto me, Write, from henceforth blessed are the dead who die in the Lord: Even so, saith the Spirit, for they rest from their labors."

Then shall the minister say, "Lord, have mercy upon us. Christ, have mercy upon us. Lord, have mercy upon us."

Then the minister may offer this prayer (this prayer can only be prayed at the saved's grave),* "Almighty God, with whom do live the spirits of those who depart hence in the Lord, and with whom the souls of the faithful, after they are delivered from the burden of the flesh, are in joy and felicity; we give Thee hearty thanks for the good examples of all those Thy servants, who, having finished their course in faith, do now rest from their labors. And we beseech Thee, that we, with all those who are departed in the true faith of Thy holy name, may have our perfect consummation and bliss, both in body and soul, in Thy eternal and everlasting glory, through Jesus Christ our Lord. Amen.

The Collect

O Merciful God, the Father of our Lord Jesus Christ, who is the resurrection and the life; in whom whosoever believeth shall live, though he die, and whosoever liveth and believeth in Him shall not die eternally; we meekly beseech thee, O Father, to raise up from the death of sin unto the life of righteousness; that when we shall depart this life we may rest in Him; and at the general

---

*This is another parenthetical added by Seymour.

resurrection on the last day may be found acceptable in Thy sight, and receive that blessing which Thy well-beloved Son shall then pronounce to all that love and fear Thee, saying, Come, ye blessed children of My Father, receive the kingdom prepared for you from the beginning of the world. Grant this, we beseech Thee, O merciful Father, through Jesus Christ our Mediator and Redeemer. Amen.

Our Father who are in heaven, hallowed be Thy name. Thy kingdom come. Thy will be done on earth, as it is in heaven. Give us this day our daily bread: and forgive us our trespasses, as we forgive them that trespass against us: and lead us not into temptation, but deliver us from evil: for thine is the kingdom, and the power, and the glory, forever. Amen.

The grace of our Lord Jesus Christ, and the love of God, and the fellowship of the Holy Ghost, be with us all evermore. Amen.

Epilogue

Today in downtown Los Angeles.
312 Azusa Street is now part of a plaza adjoining the
Japanese Cultural Center.
A plaque marks the site of the history making revival.

The Larry Martin Collection

Opportunity once passed is lost forever. There is a time when the tide is sweeping by our door. We may then plunge in and be carried to glorious blessing, success and victory. To stand shivering on the bank, timid or paralyzed with stupor, at such a time, is to miss all, and most miserably fail, both for time and for eternity. Oh, our responsibility! The mighty tide of God's grace and favor is even now sweeping by us, in its prayer-directed course. There is a river (of salvation) the streams whereof make glad the city of God (Psalm 46:4). It is time to "get together," and plunge in, individually and collectively. We are baptized "in one Spirit, into one body" (1 Cor. 12:13). Let us lay aside all carnal contentions and divisions, that separate us from each other and from God. If we are of His body, we are "one body." The opportunity of a lifetime, of centuries, is at our door, to be eternally gained or lost. There is no time to hesitate. Act quickly, lest another take thy crown. Oh, church of Christ, awake! Be baptized with power. Then fly to rescue others. And to meet your Lord.

Frank Bartleman
Gospel Tract
June, 1906

Once again America stands on the verge of a great spiritual awakening. The river is rising across the nation. Let us not allow this mighty torrent to pass us by. Pray, church, pray! May the same Spirit that flooded Azusa Street now flood every street from Pennsylvania Avenue to Wall Street to Main Street to your street. Please, God, send revival to the United States of America.

Larry Martin
2012

165

The Complete Azusa Street Library

The Life and Ministry of *William J. Seymour*
LARRY MARTIN

How Pentecost Came to Los Angeles
Frank Bartleman

THE APOSTOLIC FAITH

Pentecost Has Come

The Comforter Has Come!

WWW.AZUSASTREET.ORG

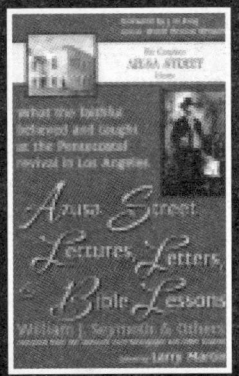

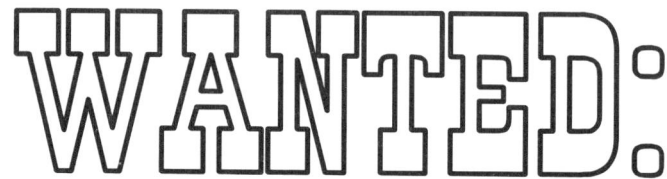

WANTED:

More Information on the Azusa Street Revival

Did any of your ancestors participate at Azusa Street?

If so, I would love to hear from you. Please send me:

- ☑ *Names*
- ☑ *Photos*
- ☑ *Stories*
- ☑ *Printed Materials*

Please help us collect and preserve the Azusa story for future generations.

Larry Martin
P.O. Box 36355
Pensacola, FL 32516
mail@drlarrymartin.org

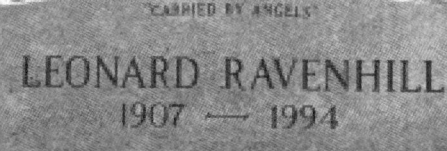

This Book Should Be Mandatory Reading for Every Serious Christian Worker!

Reuben A. Torrey

WHY GOD USED D.L. MOODY

WITH A BRIEF BIOGRAPHY OF MR. MOODY & TWO SERMONS BY THE GREAT EVANGELIST

D. L. Moody was the greatest evangelist of his generation, perhaps of all generations. He personally preached to more than 100 million people before the days of mass communication or transportation. Tens of thousands were converted by this anointed servant of God. Although mostly without formal education, Moody also wrote books, established churches and founded schools that are still training men and women for ministry.

R. A. Torrey, one of Moody's closest friends is uniquely qualified to tell the world of Moody's secrets to success with both God and man. This book will challenge and inspire every reader whose heart is praying for a closer walk with God and more effective Christian service.

Christian Life Books has added a brief biography of Moody and two of his great sermons to this reprint. It is sent out with the prayer that God will use others as he used Dwight L. Moody.

Logging some 150,000+ miles a year and often speaking with over half-a-million young people annually, Winkie Pratney has wide experience in youth work. His technical background in both science and the popular music culture has given him a unique insight to the particular needs of a media-dominated technological society, and his constant monitoring of youth trends combined with continual feedback from young people themselves has helped him interpret these for those with a vital interest in the welfare of the young. Besides annual leadership training seminars he has for three decades helped challenge and inspire young people to holy and happy living.

A frequent featured speaker and guest on national television talk shows, his audio and video-tape lectures are carried by many effective outreach ministries as part of their training. Winkie has authored more than twelve books including youth manuals like the best-selling *Youth Aflame!, Handbook For Followers Of Jesus,* books on contemporary and historical issues like *Devil Take The Youngest, Dealing With Doubt* and evangelistic and apologetic works like the contemporary devotional theology *The Nature And Character Of God.*

❖

Histories of the world's greatest revivals!

Biographies of the revivalists!

Proven principles to change the world!

❖

When the question is asked: "What hinders revival?" one of the simple answers is this: We do not have men and women who are prepared to pay the same price to preach the same message and have the same power as those revivalists of the past. Without these firm believers, the community can never be changed.

We say we want revival. But who today is prepared to live a life of absolute obedience to the Holy Spirit, tackling sin in the church as well as the streets, preaching such a message of perfection of heart and holiness of life—a message feared and hated by the religious and street sinner alike?